Probability and Purpose

A Refutation of Divine Intent

IVAN PHILLIPS

PROBABILITY AND PURPOSE

Copyright © 2025 Ivan Phillips

All rights reserved

Barley Lane Books

PO Box 5613, Buffalo Grove, IL 60089

www.barleylanebooks.com

March 25, 2025

First Edition, 2025

Edited by Koka Kliora

ISBNs: 978-1-7365783-4-6 (paperback); 978-1-7365783-5-3 (eBook)
978-1-7365783-7-7 (hardcover)

10 9 8 7 6 5 4 3 2 1

To my teachers, who taught me about truth and beauty

Contents

Preface

1	The Thesis	1
2	Argument from Evidence	15
3	Chance, Design, and Darwinian Evolution	43
4	Divine Design	71
5	The Counterargument from Design	93
6	Objections	99
7	Cosmic Fine-Tuning	135
8	Conclusion	149

Preface

I first learned about Bayesian philosophy about 15 years ago and was immediately charmed by the idea. The central premise of Bayesianism is that all beliefs are probabilistic, and that we should update our beliefs according to the evidence using Bayes' Theorem. This implies that if you rationally believe something to be true, you ought to be able to construct a good, Bayesian argument to back it up.

I believed that my naturalistic worldview was rational, and that there was no God who intentionally created humans, neither by special creation nor by some seemingly natural process. So, a few years ago, I set out to construct a Bayesian argument to match my intuitions. I expected I would find a modest probabilistic justification for naturalism. Instead, I was surprised to find the inference to naturalism was extremely strong. If the argument stands up, then there is no design at any level of biology. The argument says nothing about a deity who created evolution, with no intent for what resulted, but the argument does imply that theistic evolution, the theory that God specifically designed us by way of evolution, was effectively ruled out.

At its heart, the argument is quite simple, and I was surprised to discover that no one seemed to have constructed it—at least, not in the manner I did. So, last year, I submitted a paper on this topic to the philosophy journal, *Philosophia*. The paper was rejected, but in the best way imaginable: one of the reviewers generously wrote a five-page paper critiquing the ideas in my submission. Since my original paper was already at the journal's word limit, there was no way I could answer all the objections in any single paper. I decided to write this book instead.

My academic training has been in physics, so I am by no means an expert in probability theory, theology, or evolutionary biology. However, I hope that this argument inspires illuminating critique and productive conversation from scholars in the scientific, theological, and philosophical communities.

I wish to acknowledge Noah Greenstein and Brian Burtt for their feedback on my original journal submission. I am also indebted to my anonymous reviewer for their challenging objections. Finally, I thank my editor, Koka Kliora, for her corrections and helpful critiques.

Ivan Phillips

March 2025

1

The Thesis

"It seems to me absurd to doubt that a man may be an ardent Theist and an evolutionist. I have never been an atheist in the sense of denying the existence of a God."[1]

— *Charles Darwin*

---

[1] Letter to John Fordyce, 7 May 1879. Though Darwin's faith was weakened by his conclusions about evolution, he remained a theist of a sort. Darwin Correspondence Project, "Letter no. 12041," accessed on 26 September 2022,
   https://www.darwinproject.ac.uk/letter/?docId=letters/DCP-LETT-12041.xml

Probability and Purpose

Once upon a time, there was no more direct and intuitive proof of God than the intricate form and function of living things. We marvel at the beauty of apple blossoms and the structure of the fruit and seeds they produce, and we are compelled to awe when we observe the sophistication of even the simplest biological cell. Such observations are the bedrock of natural theology—the inference to the existence of God by seeing the general patterns in nature and human life. And so, for more than two millennia, philosophers were convinced that the best explanation for the structure of life was divine design. Then came Charles Darwin.

Long before Darwin published his book, *On the Origin of Species*, observers of nature knew that animals of different kinds had striking similarities. They also knew about evolution—that Earth's species changed over time, that there had once lived species that had since become extinct. What they lacked was a natural, mechanical theory to explain the similarities between species and their changes over time. Without such a mechanical theory, only design could explain Earth's natural history. But Darwin showed that natural selection acting on genetic variation in a population would lead to new species and new biological features. Evolutionary processes combine the power of trial and error with genetic memory. This simple mechanism tries new adaptations, new innovations, and by preserving these innovations in living populations, can build upon them.

By dethroning divine design as the explanation for the observable structure of life, Darwin defanged the most potent argument for God's existence. Today, evolutionary biology sits at the heart of biology.

The Thesis

Evolution is taught in most public schools and at all leading universities. Even the Vatican now endorses the teaching of evolutionary biology.[2]

Most atheists that I know see evolution as an argument against design, albeit not a decisive one. Evolution is not the story handed down to us in Genesis or in any other religious text. Yes, God could have created the world to look evolved, but it's not what we might have expected.[3] Evolution does not fit well with the story of a designing God. However, the prevailing opinion among theists and atheists alike is that evolutionary theory does not rule out divine design entirely. We can all imagine a designer who covertly influenced the random factors in evolution's path, knowing that such influence would guarantee humanity's existence. Who's to say that the world as we know it was not intended by a God who used evolutionary processes to bring about human life?

Thus, most people understand evolution to have merely neutralized an important argument for God's existence. Many theists both accept the science of biology and still see design in the biological world.[4]

In this book, I argue that the prevailing opinion is wrong. The atheist's intuitions of a poor fit were only the tip of the iceberg. The science of evolutionary biology does far more than neutralize the design argument

---

[2] Benedict XVI. (2007). *Meeting of The Holy Father Benedict XVI with the clergy of the dioceses of Belluno-Feltre And Treviso.* Vatican.va. 2007-07-24. Retrieved 2023-05-30.

[3] I use God, creator, and designer, interchangeably, to refer to any kind of omnipotent, omniscient designer or group of designers.

[4] Pew Research Center, Feb. 6, 2019, *The Evolution of Pew Research Center's Survey Questions About the Origins and Development.*

for God's existence—it turns it upside down. I shall argue that evolutionary biology is potent scientific proof that we were not designed by God at all. I call my argument the Counterargument from Design. In these pages, I shall explain why evolution rules out design and offer a plausible explanation for the peculiar fact that such an argument has not been formally made in the past.

At its heart, my argument is so simple that I can sketch it for you in two paragraphs. In the absence of design, in a universe that operates on blind physical chemistry, life can only come about through evolutionary processes. Compared with design, evolutionary processes are extremely limited in what they can do. Though Darwin wrote, "from so simple a beginning endless forms most beautiful and most wonderful have been, and are being, evolved," evolution makes rather narrow predictions about what kinds of life we ought to expect. Evolved life has distinctive qualities and limitations that designed life, in general, does not. Though every world where life has evolved will have very different species, we expect all evolved life to have the same sorts of properties we see on Earth. These include properties like reproductive systems, common descent, and the kind of legacy biochemistry predicted by descent with modification.

In contrast, life designed by an infinitely capable creator has no such limitations. Of course, an omnipotent God can create worlds that evolve or look evolved, but they also have infinitely more options than blind processes. If all we knew about a life-bearing world was that it was designed, there would be so many possible ways life could be, we would literally have no idea what to expect. Whereas unguided evolution *must* result in life like the kind we observe here on Earth, design predicts nothing and everything. Statistically speaking, design predicts just about anything but what we see. Indeed, when we crunch the numbers, we can show that, as much as we know anything at all, we know we were not designed.

To make the basic statistical argument clearer, consider an analogy with decks of playing cards. Suppose that I have two decks of cards. One deck of cards consists of 52 copies of the ace of hearts. The other deck is a normal, shuffled deck. At random, I place one of the two decks of cards face down in front of you. Which deck is before you?

Initially, you have no more reason to think the deck in front of you is more likely to be one deck than the other. It is 50-50. I now allow you to draw the top card from the deck. You draw the ace of hearts. What should you believe about the deck in front of you? Rationally, you ought to believe that the deck in front of you is much more likely to be the deck that consists exclusively of copies of the ace of hearts. Indeed, if you bet on the ace of hearts deck whenever the first card drawn is the ace of hearts, you will be right 52 times out of 53.

In this card game analogy, the ace of hearts represents the evolutionary pattern in natural history. If naturalism is true, if the universe is governed by chemistry that is incapable of foreseeing the future and evolution is unguided, then the pattern of life on every world will be the same. The 51 other, distinct cards in the standard deck represent alternative ways that a God might design life, generating forms of life that evolution cannot. The random choice of deck represents our ignorance about what world we live in, and the shuffling of the standard deck represents our ignorance of what a designer would do.

Of course, an infinite designer has far more than 51 alternatives to the evolutionary pattern. For every world that looks outwardly the same as our own, there are trillions, or perhaps an infinite number of alternatives, that can be created by an all-powerful designer.[5] And as the number of alternatives goes up, so does the strength of the argument. If, instead of 52-card decks, we were dealing with trillion-card decks, and you drew an ace of hearts instead of, say, the billion of clubs, you would know that you were dealing with the ace of hearts deck as much as you know anything in your experience.

If the Counterargument from Design feels counterintuitive to you, you are not alone. Even dyed-in-the-wool atheists seem to have missed the argument. Accordingly, suspicion of this argument is warranted. I expect that you, dear reader, have already formulated an objection or two of your own. In the following chapters, I will refine the argument and show where it applies and how it stands up to objections.

If the Counterargument from Design succeeds, it nonetheless has limitations. The argument does not tell us that no gods exist. It does not tell us much about gods who did not design us and do not care about our existence. But the kinds of deities that foresaw our existence and set the universe in motion to facilitate the existence of humanity specifically are ruled out by the counterargument, for that would be a type of design.

---

[5] I will discuss finite versus infinite designers in Chapter 4.

The Thesis

This book is written primarily for those who accept evolutionary biology, broadly speaking. However, I hope that my explanation of evolutionary processes will also be helpful to those who have their doubts about the mechanism of the modern synthesis of Darwinian evolution.

My thesis requires me to touch a third rail. In recent decades, creationists have promoted an alternative to evolution that they call intelligent design. The academy and the courts consider intelligent design to be a pseudoscientific front for religious creationism, and I agree. The dividing line between science and pseudoscience involves numerous criteria. Pseudoscientists refuse to engage meaningfully with their critics. Their pseudoscience makes no scientific progress over time, and when pseudoscientists fail to publish in peer-reviewed journals, they weave conspiracy theories to explain why their efforts seem to go nowhere. Intelligent design meets all the criteria for pseudoscience, and rightfully, scientists are unwilling to engage with it on equal terms. Though intelligent design does not pass muster as a science, this book is a philosophy book, and I am happy to engage with intelligent design as a philosophical notion. This engagement should not be construed as lending legitimacy to intelligent design as science. Indeed, as I shall show, intelligent design is an extremely poor theory.

The Counterargument in Context

> *"I have taken an interest in science and have been studying it for 5 years."*
> — Ivan, aged 10

I found this amusing quote in my old fifth grade creative writing workbook. Perhaps more pedantic than precocious, I was obsessed with all things scientific and technological. I passionately wanted to understand how the cosmos worked, and for as long as I can remember, I wanted to be a scientist. I religiously watched every episode of Carl Sagan's *Cosmos*, the BBC's *The Voyages of Charles Darwin*, and James Burke's *Connections*. The conflict between science and religion loomed large in these popular programs, and I naturally became quite suspicious of religious viewpoints. At the same time, I believed that theological or metaphysical questions were very important. For me, understanding the cosmos was paramount. Like most people, I wondered if some aspects of reality might require a nonphysical explanation.

By the time I was 14, I had settled on a natural picture of reality that had no need for a divine creator, let alone a God that is active in the world today. In a natural world, the fundamental laws of reality are non-mental. When electrons and photons interact, their interactions are described by physical laws that have no mental aspects to them. Under naturalism, the richness of life and thought in human minds is the result of the complex structure of the simple, mindless chemistry of fundamental particles.

The Thesis

Despite my confidence in naturalism, my interest in these deep philosophical and theological questions has always been with me. My quest for understanding the universe would carry me through my doctoral program in theoretical physics at Northwestern University. In the decades that followed, I sought out the best philosophical arguments for theism that I could find.

Over the centuries, apologists for theism have devised dozens of arguments for the existence of God, of which the argument from design is but one. The most famous of these arguments for the existence of God is the cosmological argument, which argues that all things must have a cause, and names God as the first and ultimate cause. But there are many lesser-known arguments, such as the ontological argument, the moral argument, and arguments from reports of miracles. It has even been argued that God must exist to fill the God-shaped hole in the human heart.

Recently, arguments from cosmic fine-tuning have become popular. These arguments claim that there is a delicate balance of physical forces which permits life to exist in the universe, and this balance is best explained by an intelligent designer who carefully arranged the physics of the universe to make it compatible with life. In its structure, the Fine-Tuning Argument resembles the Counterargument from Design. They are both probabilistic, evidential arguments.

For each argument for God's existence, skeptics have offered a compelling rebuttal as well as a few negative arguments of their own. The most persuasive of the skeptical arguments is the problem of evil—the claim that the gratuitous evils in the world are inconsistent with a benevolent and omnipotent God. The problem of evil is obvious and emotionally moving, and it has been contemplated since at least the time of Epicurus in the fourth century BCE, and probably since long before.

For my own part, I find theistic arguments weak or fallacious. They may act as a salve for someone looking to justify their faith in a God who hides from us, but they are hardly potent enough to convince a skeptic. After all, people do not spend millennia writing arguments for the existence of mountains or sharks. Arguments for God's existence are needed only because, if there is a God, they are so hidden as to appear nonexistent. At the same time, skeptical arguments aren't decisive either. The problem of evil is compelling if one assumes God has a morality like our own, but that is a big assumption.

Having found none of the popular arguments for God's existence compelling, I felt comfortable with my atheism. To my mind, atheism fared at least a little better in each debate, and so, holistically, atheism seemed to have a much stronger case. And atheism seemed like a better fit with the natural history of life on Earth.

All this changed for me after I formalized the Counterargument from Design. Finally, here was a single, extremely strong argument that ruled out a whole class of gods and did so based on potent scientific evidence. I could now point to a specific reason why most forms of theism can be ruled out based on scientific evidence.

The Thesis

Of course, convincing myself of something I already believed was a trivial accomplishment. Still, I had been thinking about and debating such philosophical matters for decades, and I found the structure of the Counterargument from Design to be quite novel.

Arguing from the fact of evolution to atheism is not new, of course. Darwin himself had misgivings about publishing his work, because evolution clearly implied the existence of the traditional, Christian deity was less probable. As philosopher Daniel Dennett noted in his book, *Darwin's Dangerous Idea*, evolution has impacts on many areas of philosophy.[6] Human consciousness and morality must now be viewed in a fashion consistent with Earth's natural history, and theistic and supernatural ideas do not fit well in this natural landscape.

Philosopher Philip Kitcher has argued that evolutionary biology creates an even deeper problem of evil for theism.[7] Evolutionary processes require pain and suffering of life forms on a global scale for millions of years. Is an evolved world really the most moral world a God could create?

I have known about these arguments for years, and while they carry some weight, none of them particularly resemble the Counterargument from Design. Recently I found a paper that explicitly makes use of the counterargument. Paul Draper of Purdue University wrote a paper in 1997 that was eventually published in *Philosophy of Religion: An Anthology*

---

[6] Dennett, D. C. (2014). *Darwin's Dangerous Idea: Evolution and the Meaning of Life.* United Kingdom: Simon & Schuster.
[7] Kitcher, P. (2006). *Living with Darwin: Evolution, Design, and the Future of Faith.* United States: Oxford University Press, USA.

in 2015.[8] In "Evolution and the Problem of Evil," Draper notes that evolution is much more probable under naturalism than under theism.

Just like the Counterargument from Design, Draper's argument is evidential, claiming not that theism is impossible, but rather that it is improbable in light of the evidence. Specifically, Draper argues that if life were designed, we would antecedently have expected to find obvious cases of special creation, i.e., cases of obvious design outside the natural constraints of evolutionary common descent. Special creation is much more probable under design than under natural evolution, and since the evidence shows no sign of special creation, we should infer from the fact of natural evolution that naturalism is much more probably true than theism.

However, while Draper makes note of this critical difference between evolution and design, he focuses instead on the connection between suffering and the evolutionary process. Draper claims that, even if God eschewed special creation in Earth's natural history, a benevolent God would not have arranged the connections between pain and suffering to create such vast amounts of natural evil.

Thus, the Counterargument from Design that I present in this book can be thought of as an elaboration of Draper's 1997 paper. There are three major distinctions between my argument and Draper's. The first is

---

[8] Rea, Michael, and Pojma, Louis. *Philosophy of Religion: An Anthology.* Seventh Edition, Cengage Learning, 2015.

that my argument relies a little more explicitly on Bayesian probability theory, which I will introduce in the next chapter.

The second difference is that I elaborate on the meaning of special creation. There are many ways an omnipotent designer could deviate from naturalistic evolution, and violating the pattern of common descent is but one.

Finally, I do not explicitly rely on any expectation of benevolence on the part of the designer. In traditional theism, it is argued that God is not only omnipotent and omniscient, but also perfectly good. Personally, I think the arguments for the perfect goodness of God are weak and that divine goodness is so fuzzy a concept that it makes predictions impossible. However, the Counterargument from Design does factor in the utility of life. When life evolves through natural causes, the only utility is survival. What *can* happen *does* happen, and, in nature, there is no prohibition against adversarial relationships between species. But presumably, a divine creator may possess any of an infinite set of values that differ from simple survival utility. So, while I do not assume anything about God's morality, the possibility of moral values means we would have to be epistemically very unlucky to find ourselves in a universe governed by a God who makes the world look natural.

I do not expect many committed theists to be won over by the Counterargument from Design. This is not how persuasion works. But I hope that the counterargument, and the logic of probability that drives it, will provide the reader with new perspectives. In particular, the human mind tends to think, fallaciously, that if we can devise a story in which an intelligent agent arranges some situation, then we have not only a *possible* explanation for that state of affairs but also a *likely* explanation. In truth, we must first consider all the alternative actions the agent could have taken. If an agentic theory predicts only what you have observed after you observe it, then that agentic theory does not accomplish any work.

This book is structured like the counterargument itself:

In Chapter 2, I explain the principles of argument from evidence. Specifically, I give an intuitive explanation of Bayesian inference, a potent recipe for updating one's confidence in a theory based on new evidence.

In Chapter 3, I explain how unguided evolutionary processes overcome biological challenges. I describe eight general predictions that we expect to be satisfied on any world where life evolves unguided.

In Chapter 4, I discuss infinite designers. I show that infinite designers are not bound by the same constraints as evolution and are thus capable of creating an infinity of living systems that are out of reach of unguided evolution.

With all the ingredients in place, I formally state the Counterargument from Design in Chapter 5.

In Chapter 6, I challenge the Counterargument from Design with 10 kinds of objections.

Finally, in Chapter 7, I compare the Counterargument from Design to the Fine-Tuning Argument and show why the Counterargument from Design is far stronger.

2

Argument from Evidence

"A wise man proportions his belief to the evidence."

— David Hume

The Counterargument from Design is an argument based on scientific evidence. To understand the argument, as well as the argument's assumptions and limitations, we need to understand how we ought to reason in response to evidence.

Humans have an innate, intuitive ability to learn from evidence. Infants learn their native language using the evidence they observe. With play and experience, infants learn the nature of physical objects in their environment. By the time we are in school, we are so fluent at making intuitive inferences that we think evidence speaks for itself. We think we can know automatically what is true based on direct experience and intuition. However, despite everyday appearances, evidence does not speak for itself. Evidence speaks only when placed into the context of a probabilistic argument.

A probabilistic argument is an argument that states that its conclusion is the most probably correct conclusion given the evidence. For example, when a jury finds a defendant guilty of a crime, they have succumbed to a probabilistic argument—the argument that, given the evidence, the theory that the defendant is guilty of the crime is much more probably true than the theory that the defendant is innocent. Of course, the average person may not consciously frame their judgment in terms of probability, but this is what they implicitly mean.

More specifically, each juror is entertaining two predictive theories in their mind: innocence and guilt. These two theories predict the observed evidence to greater or lesser degrees. The juror finds the defendant guilty when he or she thinks the evidence presented in court is much more probable if the defendant is guilty than if the defendant is innocent. For instance, if the defendant's fingerprints are matched at the crime scene, it is still possible that the defendant is innocent. Perhaps the defendant had some other reason to be at the scene. Perhaps the forensic matching process was faulty. Perhaps the defendant's fingerprints just happened to match the fingerprints of the true perpetrator. However, fingerprints are commonly used in criminal cases because an innocent defendant is much less likely to have their fingerprints found at a crime scene than is a guilty defendant.

In the mid-18th century, Thomas Bayes formalized this type of probability reasoning. Bayes' Theorem tells us how we ought to update our confidence in our theories when new evidence comes along. The formula compares the predictions of our theories to the observed evidence while accounting for past observations we have made.

Since its derivation two centuries ago, the Bayesian approach to probability has been controversial. In the following sections, I will explain how the method works and why the controversy exists. Along the way, I will try to clear up a few common misunderstandings about probability that often confuse newcomers to probability theory.

Bayesian Inference

My favorite way to explain Bayesian inference is with a dice game.[9] Suppose I call you on the phone and explain that I have a six-sided die and a 20-sided die in a bag. I extract one of the dice at random, placing the selected die in the palm of my hand. What is the probability that I hold the six-sided die?

At this stage, you cannot see which die I am holding. All you know is that I randomly selected between two dice, and you have no more reason to believe I selected the six-sided die than the 20-sided die. Thus, you

---

[9] Phillips, I. (2021). *Textbook Rationality: Rationality, and Why We Should Teach It in Schools*. Barley Lane Books.

estimate the probability at 50-50—that there is a 50% probability that it was the six-sided die.

Here, we can address the first confusion that arises when we begin to think about probability. Surely, the random selection has already been made, and while it is obscured from your view, I know that there is either a 0% chance or a 100% chance that the six-sided die is sitting in my palm. How can it make any sense to say that it is 50-50?

This is an excellent question for clarifying what we mean by probability. Probability is observer-dependent. The probability is indeed 0% or 100% for an agent who has perfect and direct access to the facts. If I am certain that the die in my palm is the six-sided die, then the probability for me is 100%. If there is an omniscient observer watching us play this dice game, that observer, too, will see the six-sided die in my palm and conclude the probability is 100%. However, you lack the information that we have. You know only that there was a random selection between the two dice. For you, the probability is 50-50. This kind of probability is called epistemic probability. It is a way of accounting for what you know (and what you don't know) based on the evidence you have and based on your assumptions.

I should note that the same conclusion applies even if the die was selected nonrandomly. If I intentionally pick one of the two dice but you do not know my rationale for picking dice, then you still have no more reason to think I picked the six-sided die over the 20-sided die.

Argument from Evidence

When I broach the topic of how probability applies to choices God might make, I commonly hear the objection that we do not know on what basis God would make choices or the objection that God is not making choices randomly. As with our dice game example, neither of these objections is relevant. All that is relevant here is our lack of knowledge. I dare say most theologians would argue that God chooses deliberately, but also that he chooses mysteriously. Such claims are perfectly compatible with the Counterargument from Design. All we need to admit is that we do not know how God chooses.

Let's return to our dice game. Suppose I now roll the die I selected and inform you that I rolled a three. What, now, is your estimate of the probability that I selected the six-sided die?

At this stage, it could still be either die. It is possible to roll a three on both the six-sided die and the 20-sided die. In my experience, most people initially respond by saying that they still have no idea which die was selected. But after being prompted to think about the situation and given a moment to reflect, people realize they have been given a bit more useful information. Threes are more common on the six-sided die than on the 20-sided die. That is, the six-sided-die theory predicts a higher probability of rolling a three than does the 20-sided-die theory. The symmetry between the six-sided-die theory and the 20-sided-die theory has been broken.

In fact, you can use the predictions of the two theories to precisely estimate the probability that the six-sided-die theory is correct. To do this, imagine playing our dice game 120 times. In 120 games, you expect I would randomly select each die 60 times. Of the 60 games where I select the six-sided die, you expect a three to appear 10 times. Of the 60 games where I select the 20-sided die, you expect to see just three threes. Thus, when a three appears on the first roll of the die, in 10 out of 13 cases, it will have appeared on the six-sided die, statistically speaking. Consequently, the updated probability that I selected the six-sided die is $\frac{10}{13}$, or about 77%. Because we assume one of the two theories is correct, the probabilities must add up to 100%, so the updated probability that the 20-sided-die theory was correct is $\frac{3}{13}$, or 23%.

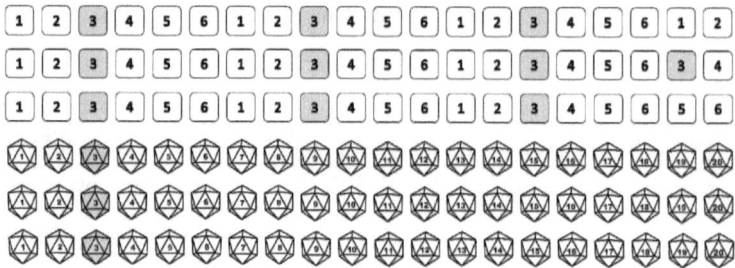

I love this teaching example because it boosts our intuition for what probabilistic reasoning is trying to do. Based on our assumptions and background knowledge, we initially concluded that there was an equal probability that either theory was correct. We then used each theory to predict the number of outcomes we expect to see that match our observation, and then we used this information to update our confidence in the respective theories.

In Bayesian terminology, you started with each theory having a *prior probability* of 50%. Your theories predicted a *likelihood* of seeing a three at $\frac{1}{6}$ and $\frac{1}{20}$, respectively. Given that you learned a three was rolled, you concluded that the *posterior probability* (*posterior*, as in *after the evidence*) that the six-sided-die theory was correct was 77%.

What should happen to your estimate if I next roll my selected die again and I roll a two?

The more times I roll the same die and get a number in the range of one through six, the more confident you will become that the six-sided-die theory is correct. If I roll my selected die a dozen more times, and each roll is six or lower, you will be more confident that I selected the six-sided die. This is because it would be quite a coincidence for the 20-sided die to roll numbers six or lower in more than a dozen trials.

Pause here to absorb this insight. What makes the six-sided-die theory a better theory is that it makes more narrow predictions than the 20-sided-die theory while still being consistent with observation. Indeed, the ability of the 20-sided-die theory to remain consistent with observations is not an asset, because the theory spreads its expectations across more possible as yet unobserved outcomes than does the six-sided-die theory.

From this, we can immediately see why a fully mysterious God is perhaps the poorest theory one could possibly devise. A mysterious God theory spreads its probability across an infinite number of possible outcomes. It is often said that the theory that predicts everything ends up predicting nothing. However, we should be clear that this is not a bias against supernatural theories, only against *vague* supernatural theories. A supernatural theory that makes narrow predictions is just as good as a natural theory that does the same. A non-mysterious God theory that made narrow predictions, if such a theory existed, could be an appealing theory.

Returning to our dice game, let's calculate what our confidence in the six-sided-die theory ought to be after rolling a three and then a two. To help us calculate our posterior probability after rolling a three, we imagined playing 120 games. To perform this task for two rolls of the die, we imagine playing 7,200 games (120 games × 60 times) and count the number of occurrences of the sequence three-two. Again, half the games are played with each die, and $\frac{10}{13}$ of the threes encountered would have been on the six-sided die. This results in 600 threes on the six-sided die and 180 threes on the 20-sided die. Of the 600 threes on the six-sided die, we expect $\frac{1}{6}$ of the subsequent rolls (100 rolls) to result in a two. Of the 180 rolls of the 20-sided die that initially produced a three, we expect $\frac{1}{20}$ of the rolls (or nine rolls) to result in a two. Thus, of 109 rolls producing the sequence three-two, 100 of them will be on the six-sided die. We conclude the probability that the six-sided die theory is correct is $\frac{100}{109}$, or about 91.7%.

As expected, a second roll of the die in the range one through six makes us more confident in the six-sided die theory. The interesting thing here is that the calculation for two rolls of the die contains the result of the calculation for one roll of the die $\left(\frac{10}{13}\right)$. This is a general property of Bayesian updating. We do not need to calculate all our probabilities from scratch each time. We can simply take the posterior probability from our last round of evidence and call them our prior probabilities in calculating how we respond to the next round of evidence. The Bayesian method is iterative. The output of the last round becomes the input for the next round.

In its simplest form, Bayes' Theorem can be written as follows:

$$P(theory|evidence) = \frac{P(evidence|theory)P(theory)}{P(evidence)}$$

This is the standard notation used in Bayesian probability. P(X) is simply shorthand for "the probability of X." The vertical bar is shorthand for "given" or "conditional on," so P(X|Y) means "the probability of X given Y" or "the probability of X conditional on Y."

Although P always refers to a probability, the probabilities in this formula have standard names that refer to their meaning:

P(theory | evidence)	The *posterior probability* of theory being true given the evidence
P(theory)	The *prior probability* that the theory is true before you evaluated the evidence
P(evidence | theory)	The *likelihood*—the probability of seeing this evidence if the theory is true
P(evidence)	The *marginal*—the probability of seeing the evidence, given the current theories in play

Let's apply Bayes' rule to our dice game. Recall, we have two theories, the six-sided-die theory and the 20-sided-die theory. I will refer to them as D6 and D20, respectively. Recall also that our prior probability for each was 50%.

$$P(D6) = 50\%$$

$$P(D20) = 50\%$$

The likelihood of rolling a three on the six-sided die is $\frac{1}{6}$:

$$P(three|D6) = \frac{1}{6}$$

Similarly, the likelihood of rolling a three on the 20-sided die is $\frac{1}{20}$:

$$P(three|D20) = \frac{1}{20}$$

The marginal or total probability of rolling a three is found by multiplying each of the likelihoods by the corresponding priors:

$$P(three) = P(D6)P(D6) + P(D20)P(D20)$$

We now have all we need to calculate the posterior probability that the six-sided die was selected is true given the evidence of rolling a three:

$$P(three) = \frac{P(D6)P(D6)}{P(three)}$$

$$= \frac{P(D6)P(D6)}{P(D6)P(D6) + P(D20)P(D20)}$$

$$= \frac{\frac{1}{6} \, 50\%}{\frac{1}{6} \, 50\% + \frac{1}{20} \, 50\%}$$

ARGUMENT FROM EVIDENCE

$$= \frac{10}{13}$$

For the second roll of the die, the likelihoods are the same, but our posterior probabilities of $\frac{10}{13}$ and $\frac{3}{13}$ become our new priors:

$$P(D6) = \frac{10}{13}$$

$$P(D20) = \frac{3}{13}$$

Putting this into the formula reproduces our second answer:

$$P(two) = \frac{P(D6)P(D6)}{P(two)}$$

$$= \frac{P(D6)P(D6)}{P(D6)P(D6) + P(D20)P(D20)}$$

$$= \frac{\frac{1}{6}\frac{10}{13}}{\frac{1}{6}\frac{10}{13} + \frac{1}{20}\frac{3}{13}}$$

$$= \frac{100}{109}$$

As you can see, the Bayesian method is iterative. Whenever you get a new piece of evidence, simply take your current estimate of the probability of each theory being true, combine it with the likelihoods (predictions) of your theories, and you get the new, updated degree of confidence you ought to hold in your theories. If your prior probability estimates are correct, you need only use Bayes' theorem and the likelihoods each theory will generate the evidence you observe. In fact, even if you did not correctly estimate your prior probabilities, by following the iterative updating process, your confidence levels will correct themselves. If you mistakenly estimate the probability of the six-sided-die theory being true is 40%, subsequent rolls of the die will correct your estimate so long as you follow Bayes' rule.

A Visual Representation of Bayesian Inference

Finally, I want to represent the Bayesian inference in this dice example graphically. This visual approach will come in handy when we consider the flaws in the Fine-Tuning Argument in Chapter 7.

When we randomly draw either the six-sided die or the 20-sided die from the bag, we cleave our expectations about the world into two pieces. Of all the universes in which we might find ourselves, 50% of those universes are worlds where the six-sided die was selected, and 50% of them are worlds in which the 20-sided die was selected.

So, let's take a horizontal bar representing 100% of our epistemic probability and divide it in half, representing the random choice between the two dice splitting our 100% prior into two segments of 50% each.

When the selected die is rolled, we further cleave each of the two halves of the epistemic probability into six and 20 smaller segments, respectively, as seen in the figure below:

WHAT CAN HAPPEN (100%)																										
6-sided die selected (50%)						20-sided die selected (50%)																			
1	2	3	4	5	6	1	2	3	4	5	6	7	8	9	10	11	12	13	14	15	16	17	18	19	20

When we observe that a three was rolled, just two pieces of this probability space survive our observation filter:

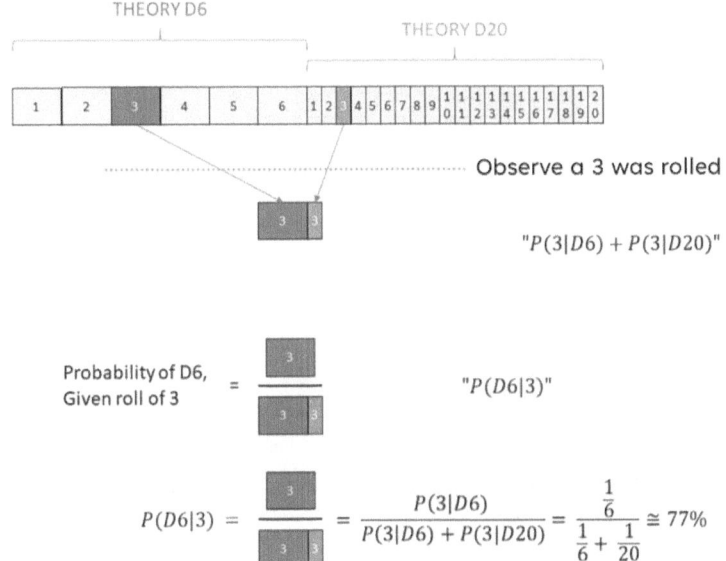

Visually, we can see that more of the prior probability from the six-sided-die theory survives the observation. Because the segment from the six-sided-die theory is larger than the segment of the 20-sided-die theory, we can infer that it is more likely that the six-sided die was extracted from the bag. Moreover, we can construct the posterior probability that the six-sided-die theory is true, given that a three was rolled, by computing the ratio of the size of the six-sided die segment to the sum of the segments of both theories.

This graphical representation of the inference is nothing more than a kind of scaling up of the dice diagram—instead of displaying 120 games, it is as if we are displaying the proportional outcome of billions of games.

Observer Selection Effects

As finite beings, we rarely have the whole story. There is plausibly so much in the cosmos to which we are completely blind. To quote Shakespeare, "There are more things in heaven and Earth, Horatio, than are dreamt of in your philosophy." What kinds of limits does this place on our probabilistic judgments?

Consider three hypothetical lotteries. The first lottery, TRILLION, rolls a trillion-sided die and prints the resulting number on each ticket. When you buy a ticket from TRILLION, you can get any number from one up to 1,000,000,000,000. The second lottery, SIX, rolls a six-sided die, and any ticket you buy will be numbered in the range one through six. The third lottery, MINI-TRILLION, like the first, rolls a trillion-sided die, but the lottery operators only print tickets if the number is six or less. From our perspective as ticket buyers, there is no distinction between SIX and MINI-TRILLION. In both lotteries, your lottery ticket will be numbered in the range one through six. Yet, the difference between TRILLION and the two other lotteries will be easy to detect. If you buy a lottery ticket and the number on the ticket is six or less, then you can statistically infer that you almost certainly bought the ticket from SIX or from MINI-TRILLION.

The printing of the tickets creates an additional filter, not directly imposed by our observation of the world but by our ability to observe the world. It is a filter on who can make observations—an *observer selection effect*. Observer selection effects discard the unobservable parts of the prior probability while retaining the overall prior probability.[10] In visual terms, it looks like the figure below.

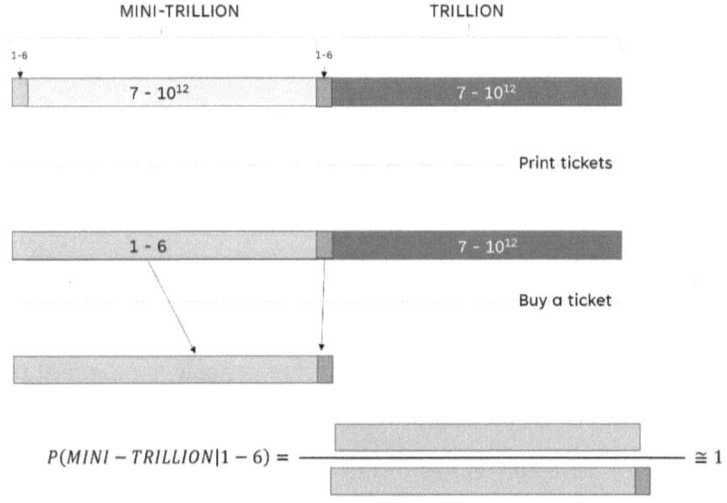

The observer selection effect is profoundly important to probabilistic judgments we may make about design and evolution. It isn't what possibilities *exist*, but what possibilities we can observe. Scientific naturalism is a collection of statements about what cannot happen and what cannot be observed. In contrast, anything is possible with God. Miracles, for example, are violations of physical prohibitions. Under theism, there is nothing we could not observe tomorrow. Thus, there is an important asymmetry between physical theories and theistic ones. Since nothing is prohibited, a much greater part of the prior remains after

---

[10] For an explanation of observer selection effects as they apply to design arguments, see Sober, E. *The Design Argument.* Cambridge University Press, 2018.

we account for the observer selection effect. This, in its turn, dilutes the fraction of the prior corresponding to whatever we eventually observe.

From Bayes' Theorem to Bayesian Epistemology

The probabilistic inferences I have described so far follow straightforwardly from the assumptions that were laid down in the description of the game or lottery. To mathematically prove Bayes' theorem, we would first assume that we know which theories are possible and that these theories are mutually exclusive. We would also assume the probabilities do not change and that we can state the likelihoods of seeing evidence in the possible theories. In our dice example, we assumed that one of two mutually exclusive theories explained the rolls of the die. Either the six-sided-die theory is true or the 20-sided-die theory is true. With these assumptions, the conclusions follow from our definitions. Reality, of course, is generally much more complex, not just because our data may be more ambiguous, but because we do not know all the theories in advance. In the sciences, we have not even dreamt up all the possible theories that might explain the data. Moreover, given the theories in our possession, we often have difficulty making precise predictions.

Another thorny issue is the question of prior probabilities. In our dice game, we set our priors to 50-50 because a random selection of one of the two dice was one of the preset rules of the game. In science and philosophy, our choice of prior probability is never as clear. When we have a lot of statistics and background information, prior probabilities can sometimes be estimated scientifically. For example, we can sometimes estimate the prior probability that a patient has a disease based on the average prevalence of the disease in the general population. In philosophy, the estimation of prior probabilities is more difficult. We cannot measure the prevalence of designed versus evolved worlds to calibrate our priors.

Despite these challenges, the application of Bayesian methods to fuzzier, real-world situations has become commonplace in both science and philosophy. Today, the leading theory of scientific inference is Bayesian.[11] To quote Michael Strevens:

> *Bayesian confirmation theory… is the predominant approach to confirmation in late twentieth century philosophy of science. It has many critics, but no rival theory can claim anything like the same following. The popularity of the Bayesian approach is due to its flexibility, its apparently effortless handling of various technical problems, the existence of various a priori arguments for its validity, and its injection of subjective and contextual elements into the process of confirmation in just the places where critics of earlier approaches had come to think that subjectivity and sensitivity to context were necessary.*

There will no doubt be some readers who reject the theoretical underpinnings of the Counterargument from Design on the basis that they reject Bayesian epistemology or perhaps even the very notion that probability can be applied to questions about God. This is a complex topic, and a full, mathematical treatment of these issues is beyond the

---

[11] Michael Strevens, Notes on Bayesian Confirmation Theory, 2017. https://www.strevens.org/bct/

scope of this book. However, I shall return to this topic when I consider objections to the Counterargument from Design in Chapter 6.

Gaps in Evidence

Science deniers love to point to gaps in our scientific understanding of the world, with the implication that these gaps undermine the science and leave room for supernatural intervention. Evolutionary biology has frequently been attacked in this way, and it is important to understand why such critiques don't hold water.

Our understanding of the world will never be complete. There is an infinite number of theories compatible with any finite set of data, and even if we had access to every possible clue, we could not fit all that information in our heads. Consequently, we will always have gaps in evidence and in our theoretical understanding. If we are to preserve the notion that we can have confidence in theories, that we can have knowledge at all, we need to understand how we can justify our confidence in the face of missing pieces of the puzzle.

A jigsaw puzzle makes a good first analogy. The two jigsaw puzzles below (Figure 1 and Figure 2) are missing pieces. Because so many pieces are missing from the first puzzle, we cannot infer the existence of an animal in the image. There are too many gaps.

Figure 1

But the puzzle in Figure 2 is also missing many pieces, and yet the completed puzzle will more probably depict a tiger. One may object that tigers have eyes and the part of the puzzle depicting the tiger's eyes has not yet been solved. But this objection cannot be sustained because the solved part of the tiger picks out a very narrow set of possibilities. Simply put, if the depiction were not that of a tiger, we wouldn't expect to see the parts of a tiger in the partially solved puzzle. We could be wrong in our assessment, but we are probably right.

Figure 2

We can apply similar logic to the deliberations of jurors. Imagine that we are judge and jury looking into the overnight theft of famous emeralds from a safe in a museum. The police have arrested two suspects, and prosecutors have brought them each to their own trial.

Defendant #1–Ann: Prosecutors say they have evidence that Ann visited the museum during opening hours, and she was caught on CCTV admiring the emeralds while they were on public display.

Defendant #2–Bob: Bob's fingerprints and DNA were found on the door of the safe. He was identified as being near the vault by eyewitnesses and on CCTV cameras. The police found Bob at home, holding the emeralds and in possession of a book on cracking museum safes.

ARGUMENT FROM EVIDENCE

In reviewing the prosecutor's cases, it seems that the case against Ann is very weak. The theory that Ann is guilty predicts evidence, such as fingerprints, DNA, and CCTV evidence, that investigators did not find. Almost every museum visitor who views the emeralds will be captured on CCTV admiring them, so the fact that Ann was so observed fails to distinguish Ann from the typical, innocent museum visitor. If the prosecutor wants to justify the claim that Ann committed the burglary, they must present evidence predicted by the "Ann is guilty" theory. Thus, there are *gaps in the evidence* that make the prosecutor's case against Ann untenable.

In contrast, the case against Bob looks almost airtight. Any reasonable judge and juror would find Bob guilty. The "Bob is guilty" theory predicts very rare evidence (fingerprints and DNA on the safe, the gems at Bob's home) that we would not likely expect if Bob were not guilty.

Yet, Bob's defense attorney makes a passionate appeal. The defense argues that the prosecutors do not know how Bob traveled from his home to the museum and back again. Did Bob take the bus, a train, or call a cab? Did Bob get a ride from a friend?

The defense argues that despite the mass of incriminating evidence against Bob, there is still a *gap in the theory and understanding* of the prosecution. The prosecution does not know how Bob traveled between his home and the crime scene, so the defense argues that the entire case against Bob should be thrown out of court.

Why does the gap in Ann's case suffice to justify her acquittal while the gap in Bob's case is unpersuasive?

There is a high *prior probability* that Ann is innocent because the innocence prior is high for everyone who visits the museum during opening hours and admires the emeralds. To rationally persuade us that Ann is guilty, the prosecution must present incriminating evidence—the kind of evidence that is likely if Ann is guilty but very unlikely otherwise. And, since the prosecution presents no such incriminating evidence, there is insufficient reason to alter our prior probability.

Meanwhile, the posterior probability of Bob's innocence drops dramatically when all the incriminating evidence is accounted for. It is extraordinarily improbable that all this evidence against Bob would have been observed had he been innocent, but relatively likely if Bob were guilty. Hence, the *posterior probability* that Bob is guilty is very high.

Bob's defense claims that there is a gap in the prosecutor's theory. In Bayesian terms, the defense is claiming that if Bob were guilty, it is very likely that the prosecution would know precisely how Bob traveled to and from the scene of the crime. Since the prosecutors do not know this, the gap appears where it ought not, says Bob's defense counsel.

Of course, the flaw in the defense's argument is that Bob's guilt does not imply the prosecution will know everything about Bob's life history. The prosecution need not know details about how Bob traveled, what TV programs he watched that evening, or what he had for breakfast.

That is, the kinds of gaps highlighted by the defense are expected, even if the prosecution's theory is correct. If Bob's breakfast were a necessary ingredient in the prosecution's theory of his guilt, then that missing evidence and missing theoretical understanding would undermine the prosecution's case.

This court example mirrors our jigsaw puzzle example. The case against Ann is like the first jigsaw puzzle wherein no pattern is detected. The case against Bob resembles the second jigsaw puzzle in which a tiger is clearly identifiable, even if pieces of the puzzle are still missing.

Fine-Tuning

Bayes' Theorem formally expresses the common-sense idea that we should judge theories according to the degree that their predictions match reality. When two theories are both compatible with our observations, the theory that strongly prefers the evidence we have observed beats a theory that spreads its predictions across more unobserved alternatives.

When our pet theory is on the losing end of a Bayesian inference, it is often tempting to rescue our theory by fine-tuning it just enough to keep up with our competitor. This is what theists are doing when they claim God created a world that appears evolved. Evolved life is not what they expected, but they subsequently fine-tuned their theory of God so it is now a theory in which we are dealing with the kind of God who would make life appear evolved. Because their new version of God predicts an evolved ecosystem, both design and unguided naturalism make precisely the same predictions. "It's a tie!" they exclaim.

If there were nothing wrong with rescue by fine-tuning, then the loser in any epistemic contest could simply redefine their theory to escape refutation. That is, if this loophole is sustained, then no argument from evidence could ever succeed. Let's look more closely and see why this move doesn't work.

Suppose that Bob's defense counsel makes a last-minute appeal. Bob's defense lawyer argues that his client has been framed in a powerful criminal conspiracy. To frame Bob, the conspirators have faked the witnesses, video evidence, DNA evidence, and fingerprints. They paid off the police to place the emeralds at Bob's house when he was arrested. In pushing this conspiracy theory, Bob's attorney has fine-tuned the "Bob is innocent" theory in such a way that it now predicts the very same evidence as the prosecution's theory. The new theory is "Bob is innocent by way of being framed by conspirators," a sub-theory of the "Bob is innocent" theory. Since both theories now make the same predictions, the result is a draw, and the prosecution's theory is no better than that of the defense.

Clearly, something has gone very wrong. No judge or jury would be convinced by the defense's claim, and yet the predictions of the theories are nearly identical. If the defense's strategy were effective, probabilistic inference would be doomed because advocates for a losing theory could just propose a fine-tuned version of their original theory that happens to make the same predictions.

To see why this loophole does not work, we need to consider our initial prior probability. Suppose the jury initially assigned a 99% prior probability to the theory that Bob was innocent:

Argument from Evidence

$$P(guilty) = 0.01$$

$$P(innocent) = 0.99$$

They then updated their posterior probability based on the evidence presented by prosecutors. Suppose that the evidence presented in court has a high likelihood for the guilty theory but only one in 10,000 odds if the client is innocent:

$$P(guilty) = 0.25$$

$$P(innocent) = 0.00001$$

Then their posterior would be

$$P(E) = \frac{P(guilty)P(E|guilty)}{P(guilty)P(guilty) + P(innocent)P(E|innocent)}$$

$$= \frac{0.01 \cdot 0.25}{0.01 \cdot 0.25 + 0.99 \cdot 0.00001}$$

$$= 99.6\%$$

When the defense updates their theory of innocence to innocence by way of being framed in a conspiracy, they are actually splitting the original innocence theory into two parts:

$$P(innocent) = P(innocent\ by\ conspiracy)$$
$$+ P(innocent\ by\ other\ means)$$

Presumably, most people who are innocent of this crime are innocent by other means, such as by way of never having visited the museum, never having seen the vault, not having the means to commit the crime, not having the motive to commit the crime, and so on. That is, the prior probability of innocence by conspiracy is an extremely small part of the whole prior:

$$P(\text{innocent by conspiracy}) \ll P(\text{innocent by other means})$$

In fact, if the likelihood of seeing the prosecution's evidence in the case of innocence is small ($P(\text{innocent}) = 0.00001$), then it must be that the prior probability of being innocent by way of conspiracy is less than that likelihood:

$$P(\text{innocent by conspiracy}) < 0.0001$$

Even if we are generous and assume that

$$P(\text{innocent by conspiracy}) = 0.0001$$

Bayes' theorem still yields about the same result as before:

$$P(E) = \frac{P(guilty)P(E|guilty)}{P(guilty)P(guilty) + P(\text{innocent by other means})P(\text{innocent by other means}) + P(\text{innocent by conspiracy})P(E|\text{innocent by conspiracy})}$$

$$= \frac{0.01 \cdot 0.25}{0.01 \cdot 0.25 + 0.9899 \cdot 0.00001 + 0.00001 \cdot 0.25}$$

$$= 99.5\%$$

Thus, the reason the loophole fails is that, when you fine-tune a theory to predict the observed data after the fact, you reduce the prior probability for the fine-tuned theory by the same amount. When the defense narrows their theory to one in which their client was framed, they also reduce the prior probability that their theory was true by the same factor.

Fine-tuning is not always the wrong thing to do. Every successful scientific theory has been fine-tuned to match experimental observations. But the reason that this works is that the fine-tuned theory makes even narrower predictions than before. When we fine-tuned Sir Isaac Newton's theory of gravity by updating the gravitational constant, we made definite predictions in response. When we fine-tuned Darwin's theory of evolution by natural selection to accommodate Mendel's genetics, the theory made new and testable predictions about the shared genetic inheritance of different species.

However, when theists fine-tune their theory of God by claiming that God 2.0 designed us by evolution, they make no new predictions at all. God 2.0 is entirely parasitic on the natural theory of evolutionary biology.

Summary

When we infer confidence in our theories from evidence, we ought to prefer theories that make narrow predictions over theories that make less specific predictions. When two theories are logically consistent with our observation, Bayes' Theorem tells us how much we should update our confidence in our theories given the narrowness of the predictions of each theory.

Our dice game demonstrates just how powerful our reasoning can be, even when there are gaps in our knowledge. When a die is rolled, the outcome is not as random as it appears to us. If we knew the precise orientation of the die at the start, forces imparted to the die by the roller, mass of the die, height of the die above the table, elasticity of the tabletop, and so on, then we could predict the outcome of the roll before the die leaves the roller's hand. Yet, our ignorance of such details does not impair our statistical inference, so long as the roller is not systematically cheating. Indeed, even if the dice are not completely fair, our inference will still succeed. So long as the likelihoods are still approximately correct, our inference will continue to be valid.

This power is why the inference to evolutionary biology is so robust. We do not know the details of the history of biological mechanisms. Most species leave no trace in the fossil record, and soft tissue such as hominid brains or ancient DNA do not survive the eons. There are details about the process of evolution that we do not yet fully understand. But these gaps in our knowledge do not invalidate the inferences we have made from the evidence we possess.

Finally, one cannot rescue a losing theory solely by redefining it to match the evidence. A fine-tuned theory can ultimately prevail, but only if it makes better predictions than its competitors.

3

Chance, Design, and Darwinian Evolution

"Evolution thus is merely contingent on certain processes articulated by Darwin: variation and selection."

— *Ernst Mayr*

Do you really believe all the beauty we see in the natural world is there by chance? This is the question that believers in divine design typically ask when confronted with the scientific picture of Earth's natural history. In asking such a question, they equate evolutionary biology with random chance. Here I will explain the difference between evolution and pure chance, but I also wish to explain why design seemed like a more plausible theory before Darwin.

Biological organisms stay alive through complex mechanisms such as respiration, feeding, cell division, reproduction, locomotion, and sensory input. These mechanisms have multiple components that need to work together as a coordinated whole. For example, all living cells store their genetic code in the cell nucleus. Translating the genetic code into proteins relies on a sophisticated dance wherein enzymes transcribe segments of DNA into messenger RNA molecules. These RNA transcriptions migrate outside the cell nucleus and land on ribosomes that convert them into their corresponding proteins. Each of the participants in this mechanism has a very specific structure, without which the choreography would not work. If the parts cannot work together, then none of the parts has a reason to exist. What explains this coordination?

Technology designed by humans frequently exhibits this kind of complexity. An internal combustion engine requires the coordinated construction of the engine block, piston, camshaft, fuel valves, electronic ignition, and so on. Engine technology is possible because human designers foresee the function of each component, and design and manufacture the components accordingly. Clearly, the complexity in nature resembles, at least superficially, the complexity in human designs. If there were no known natural mechanism for creating this sort of coordination, the only natural alternative would be pure chance. Let's begin by examining why pure chance seems like a less probable explanation than design.

Solving a Maze Puzzle

To assemble a design, we must take the right steps in the right sequence. In this way, engineering the recipe for a design is like solving a maze puzzle. Consider the simple maze in Figure 3.

Figure 3–A simple maze

Solving this maze means finding the correct series of turns and movements such that we can enter at the top arrow and exit at the bottom arrow. The typical human mind finds this maze easy to solve when we can see the plan of the maze from above. Some people can spot the correct path through the maze in a few seconds and without much deliberate effort. But all of us can exploit heuristics, like recognizing dead ends and remembering them long enough to find a workable path through the maze.

The maze becomes more difficult to solve when we cannot see the entire plan from above. If our maze represented the layout of an unfamiliar supermarket, it would take us a little longer to find the exit by walking the aisles than if we had a map. To find the supermarket checkout, we would make use of our ability to look ahead in the aisle we are walking in and see the shelves and their contents. For example, we might learn that we cannot exit the store if we turn left at the eggs; instead, we must turn right and head towards the breakfast cereals.

Mazes become yet more challenging for us to solve when the walls of the maze all look the same. When the walls are indistinguishable, we need to internally keep track of which turning points we have encountered and which choices fail to find the exit. Still, a maze as simple as the one pictured above would not tax our memory very much.

Figure 4 shows the same maze with a grid to help us count steps and track movement in the maze.

Figure 4—The maze with a grid

If a person with a lamp were navigating their way through this maze without the aid of a map, they would have an advantage over their friend who is trying to do so in total darkness. A navigator who cannot see must touch the walls to know where they are. Meanwhile, a maze navigator who can see ahead need not walk to the end of every corridor to recognize it as a dead end. This reduces the number of steps they must take as well as the amount of information they must remember. The navigator who can see the path ahead can skip all steps into the boxes marked with an E in Figure 5.

Figure 5–The maze with visible dead ends marked with an E

Let's make this maze even more challenging. In addition to turning out the lights, suppose there is radiation in the maze which neutralizes memory formation. Navigators can neither see nor remember the turns they have taken. For simple mazes like ours, there is a trick that navigators can employ. By sticking to the left wall or the right wall, a navigator will always be able to find an exit that is on the outside of the maze. So long as the exit is on the boundary and not somewhere in an interior part of the maze (e.g., is not a trapdoor or a stairway leading out of the interior), walking along the left or right wall will allow the navigator to escape without remembering the route taken.

Finally, consider a maze that is harder still. Suppose that there is no lighting and that touching the walls is deadly. Now, a navigator must correctly guess the entire sequence of steps and turns they must take before they even enter the maze. If the navigator randomly picks their choice of turn and gets lucky, they can take as few as 42 steps through the maze, making only 16 turns. However, any navigator who cannot see and cannot touch the walls has a huge number of possible routes from which to guess, and they must guess correctly on their first try. At any point in the sequence, the navigator can take a step north, south, east or west. Assuming they will choose a path with no backtracking, they have three choices at any point in their prearranged route. If all that the navigator knew ahead of time is that it would take at least 42 moves to get to the exit, there are 3^{42} or about 10^{20} possible routes to guess from. Even if it took only one second to take each step on a chosen route, it would, on average, take longer than the age of the universe to find the exit, and around a hundred billion billion navigators would die in the process.

Thus, even this simple maze presents a virtually insurmountable challenge for chance alone, assuming chance equates to instantly guessing the entire sequence in advance of entering the maze. In even the simplest living cell, there are numerous maze analogues that have been solved, most of them far more complex than our example, and nature arrived at these solutions in mere millions of years. When questioners ask how anyone can believe that life arose by chance, this is the kind of chance to which they refer—nature making a blind guess for the solution to maze-like problems. Consequently, we can see why it seems intuitive to suppose that nature had help.

We can use Bayes' Theorem to compare our two theories about the maze and put the intuition in mathematical terms. Suppose we have observed that our deadly maze was traversed in less than two minutes. There are two theories that can explain the traversal:

Chance: The maze was traversed by a blind agent that randomly guessed a path through the maze.

Design: The maze was traversed by a single agent with the intent to traverse the maze and capable of seeing ahead and remembering dead ends.

Suppose we initially knew only that the maze was traversed, but not how long it took to traverse the maze. We might then assume that these two theories are equally probable:

$$P(C) = P(D) = 50\%$$

In this expression, C refers to the chance theory and D to the design theory.

When we learn that the traversal took only 120 seconds, we obtain new and relevant information. We can estimate the likelihood of completing the traversal in 120 seconds in both theories. Design is the easier likelihood to compute. Any simple strategy for intelligently navigating the maze will exit un under 120 moves, so the likelihood is approximately 1:

$$P(D) \cong 1$$

Probability and Purpose

Traversing the maze by randomly guessing a predetermined path is almost certainly going to fail. Of the 10^{20} permutations, there is only one path through this maze without backtracking, so the probability of guessing the correct path is approximately:

$$P(C) \cong \frac{1}{10^{20}} = 10^{-2}$$

Educated guessing can increase the probability somewhat because this simplified calculation excludes only immediate backtracking and does not exclude walking in circles or backing out of the maze via the entrance. The exact probability calculation is not as important as getting a relative estimate, and whether the probability is 10^{-2} or 10^{-10} matters little for our purposes.

Plugging these priors and likelihoods into Bayes' Theorem tells us that our confidence in design should be very high after performing this analysis:

$$P(\text{rapid traversal})$$
$$= \frac{P(D)P(\text{rapid traversal}|\text{design})}{P(D)P(\text{rapid traversal}|D) + P(C)P(\text{rapid traversal}|C)}$$
$$= \frac{1 \times 50\%}{1 \times 50\% + 10^{-20} \times 50\%}$$
$$= 99.999999999999999999\%$$

Correspondingly, the posterior probability that a blind navigator walked through the maze in 120 steps is tiny—about 1 in 10^{20}.

To this day, creationists and advocates for intelligent design make arguments that mistake evolutionary theory for pure chance. Astrophysicist Fred Hoyle once suggested that the claim that evolution can explain the Earth's species is akin to the hypothetical theory that a tornado could pass through a junk yard and assemble a 747 jetliner. Of course, the tornado in this hypothetical theory is a stand-in for a completely blind process of random guessing. If creationists and critics such as Hoyle are wrong, there must be something that distinguishes evolution from pure chance.

Evolving a Solution to the Maze

In our thought experiment, the agent who is trying to guess a path through the maze already has the intention of traversing the maze. If we want a more accurate depiction of nature, we need to take intention out of our picture. In evolutionary biology, there is only one thing that could be described as useful: survival. It is not that nature has any explicit goal of survival. It is a simple tautology—species that do not survive vanish, while species that survive persist.

Recall that the walls of our maze are invisible and deadly. A single agent cannot afford to make even one mistake. But evolution can bypass this problem with reproduction. If the agent can reproduce, it can afford to fail from time to time while still preserving its genetic code in its offspring. While it takes time to breed a population, the genes that define that population will go on to survive.

Let's imagine that, instead of a single agent walking through the maze, there is a multitude of simple life forms with a genetic code. This population of life forms is born outside the maze and possesses a genetic code that instructs it to take the first step into the maze. That is, when these life forms reach maturity, they occupy the first square in the maze (Figure 6).

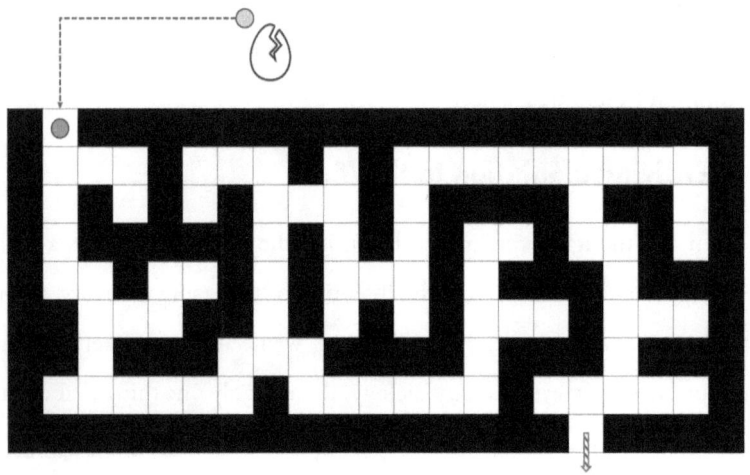

Figure 6–Maze with a simple life form that is born outside the maze, and which matures by following a genetic code that walks it into the first square

These imaginary life forms reproduce themselves. The adults in the first square have children that appear outside the maze, and these children mature by following their genetic instructions. In this case, the instructions cause them to take a single step into that first square.

Now, suppose that each time an offspring is born, there is a small chance that its genetic code is modified or augmented. Suppose also that such rare genetic mutations cause it to take an additional step into the maze during its maturation. If that second step is to the south, the individual will mature into the second square in the maze (see Figure 7). But if the mutation instructs the individual to walk east or west, they will hit the wall and die.

Figure 7–The original life form and its mutant offspring, which takes an extra step into the maze as it matures

Thus, as generations of this life form reproduce and mutate, some will have advantageous genetic traits and others will have deleterious traits. The mutants that survive will go on to populate another square in the maze, eventually producing mutant children of their own. In this analogy, each square in our maze corresponds to a different environmental niche. Each dot in the maze is a species with genetic instructions to navigate to that square in the maze. After many generations and mutations, the entire maze will be populated with species, as shown in Figure 8.

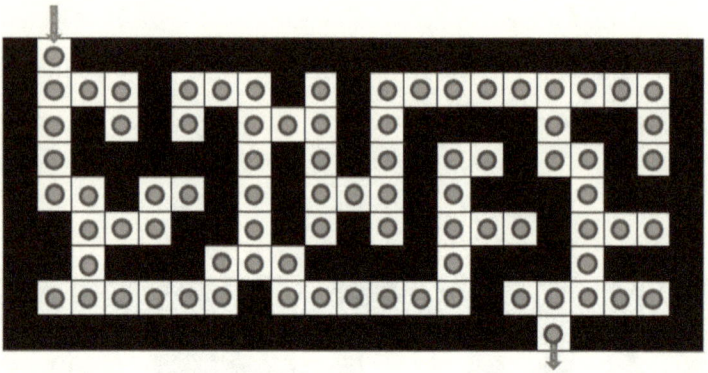

Figure 8–After many generations and mutations, the entire maze is filled with species that mature into their respective squares

This evolutionary process is more costly and time-consuming than intelligent design. It takes time for a population to replicate, multiply, and undergo rare mutations. It also costs the lives of many individual agents as they encounter the deadly walls of the maze. Another key difference between design and evolution is that, when the exit square of the maze is finally populated, there will remain populations of agents living and reproducing within the maze. This evolutionary process had no intent at all, let alone the intent to find the unique solution at the end of the maze. Nonetheless, so long as populations can survive within the maze, they will do so.

Let's estimate how long this evolutionary process will take to find a solution to this maze. The total time will depend on the breeding rate and mutation rate. In the case of single-celled life, like bacteria, populations can double every few hours. In the case of single-celled life, our maze might represent a new, simple biochemical pathway for digesting food or repairing a cell membrane. If useful mutations appear in the population every week, then it will take approximately one week for a population to establish itself in a new square. It will then take only 42 weeks to populate the entire maze. This is far better than the completely random guessing algorithm which we computed would take longer than the age of the universe to find a solution. 42 weeks is also much longer than the 42 seconds it would take for an intelligent agent, but evolution is not thought to have created all life on Earth in under six days. Life has been evolving on Earth for approximately 3.8 billion years.

Why Are There Still Monkeys?

A common question from creationists is, "If we evolved from monkeys, why are there still monkeys?" For anyone who has not thought much about evolution, this is a good question. Are humans not better than monkeys? Why haven't we replaced monkeys?

Our maze thought experiment explains why this is so. Evolution has no intent to create better or more intelligent life forms. It creates different life forms, and the genetic code of those life forms persists if they are successful survivors in their niche. When a species evolves into a new niche, it does not necessarily destroy the niche in which its ancestors live. So, when human ancestors evolved away from monkeys, finding ways to live on the ground instead of exclusively in the trees, that left plenty of opportunity for monkeys to continue thriving in the trees.

Of course, sometimes, a new mutation can cause one species to replace another. A more aggressive species of lion might outcompete another species in the same niche. Eventually, the populations themselves come to define what niches exist. Once there is a food chain with predators consuming prey, the existence of predators depends on the existence of a stable population of prey. As species evolve, they often alter the structure of the metaphorical maze. To make my maze a more apt analogy for life on Earth, I would need to account for multiple populations of species living within each square, and for changes in the maze that are caused by geological or environmental changes. For example, ice ages and widespread volcanic activity would equate to changes to the layout of the maze.

Returning to our Bayesian analysis, we now want to ask, given that agents appear at the exit of the maze within, say, three years, what is the relative likelihood of intelligent design versus evolution?

Since our evolutionary algorithm and intelligent agency can both easily find the exit of the maze in 42 weeks, the test of whether the exit can be found within three years does little to distinguish between the two theories. Expressing this in terms of intelligent design and evolution of life on Earth, we might say that, given that evolutionary biology and intelligent design can both create the species we see in 3.8 billion years, what is the relative likelihood of intelligent design and blind evolution?

Since both evolution and intelligent design can get the job done in billions of years, it might seem like probability theory applied to this particular question does not reveal much. Yet, it seems relevant that evolution takes billions of years while design can take less than six days. An intelligent designer with intent to create complex life need not take billions of years. Indeed, in the story of Genesis, God creates humans overnight. If, instead, we ask which theory better explains life, given that evidence tells us that it took millions of years for humans to arise, evolution is a far better theory.

Similarly, if the goal of creation is human agents, there is no need to design human-adjacent species like chimpanzees, gorillas, or monkeys. If humans are designed–if humans were the end goal–why are there monkeys at all?

Evolution requires that there be monkeys and chimps, or something like them. Design does not. Evolution requires that the maze be teeming with life. Design does not.

The Minimum Ingredients of Evolution

In our maze thought experiment, evolution's solution to the maze puzzle begins with a single replicating life form. On Earth, even the simplest replicating bacterium is a mechanical wonder, consisting of millions of interacting parts. If it were impossible to explain complex cells with evolutionary algorithms, then we would need to explain the improbable starting point of the first replicating cell. Fortunately, the evolutionary algorithm is general and can apply to even the simplest chemical replicator.

Evolution has three ingredients: reproduction, mutation (or variation), and natural selection. Reproduction ensures that the information a species has acquired over its evolutionary history is preserved. Reproduction is a form of memory, allowing evolution to remember solutions to biological challenges from one generation to the next. Reproduction also creates a larger population that will be more resilient in the face of accidents and bad luck. Consider the mouse. Mice are a successful species, reproducing quickly and adapting to diverse environments across the globe. Every mouse contains the genetic recipe to create another mouse. All that nature needs to make new mice is food, shelter, and some partner mice for breeding.

The mutation, or variation, allows a few members of each population within a species to try out new biological recipes. Often, this variation is unlucky, resulting in offspring that are less well adapted to their environmental niche. Yet so long as the population is adequate, a species can afford to lose members to unlucky variations.

Finally, natural selection supplies the whole system with information about the environment and which niches are survivable. Selection is a kind of learning from the environment. Every population has some genetic variation, either because they have a random selection of their parents' genes or because of mutations. The individuals of a species that are statistically disadvantaged in their niche die out through starvation, predation, or disease. Over time, favorable combinations of genes and mutations become predominant in the population.

Given these ingredients, evolution will work, no matter what the molecular details. In Earth's living species, genetic information is primarily stored in DNA. On alien worlds, evolved life may use some other molecule or mechanism to store genetic information. Yet so long as these alien biologies have replication and mutation, natural selection will give them the ability to evolve.

Chance, Design, and Darwinian Evolution

The bacteria we see today are the heirs to a vast amount of evolutionary development. The first three billion years of life on Earth consisted of single-celled life. Single-celled life replicates far more rapidly than multicellular animals, so those three billion years saw vast numbers of generations of bacteria. The first living cells were surely far less sophisticated than what we see today. Nonetheless, even the simplest replicating cell is probably highly complex. How did the first cells arise?

Scientists usually consider the question of how life began as quite separate from the question of how replicating life evolved into what we see today. Traditionally, Darwin is thought to have addressed the latter question, leaving open the mystery of how life first began. The process of creating life from non-life is called abiogenesis. Thus far, there is no scientific consensus on how the first life formed, but there are several hypotheses.

As with early cellular life, the chemistry of abiogenesis is probably not fossilized. Having no bones, simple cells or chemical channels are unlikely to be preserved in sedimentary rocks that are billions of years old. Decoding the mystery of how life formed will be a great scientific challenge. However, abiogenesis is an active scientific field because we have suggestive lines of evidence and the ability to perform laboratory experiments.

Scientists studying abiogenesis have zeroed in on a chemical process called autocatalysis. Some chemical reactions propagate themselves, creating a weak form of reproduction. This kind of reproduction is simple and lacks the sophisticated error checking that takes place in a modern cell. However, autocatalyzing processes still possess the basic ingredients for evolutionary development. They reproduce imperfectly and face selection in the form of environmental factors that affect population and chemical stability.

Researchers continue to experiment and attempt to replicate some of these chemical pathways. However, it is not surprising that we have yet to replicate this step in the lab. Nature may have taken a hundred million years to find the right chemical pathway using a natural laboratory the size of an oceanic trench. We humans have been experimenting for a few decades with a few cubic meters of experimental material.

Abiogenesis is not a gap that causes a problem for the Counterargument from Design. We do not expect to have direct evidence that tells us precisely how life first emerged from non-living material. We also have no proof that such a transition is impossible. Indeed, we have a compelling theory that might explain the transition.

General Predictions of Evolution

To place any theory into the context of Bayesian arguments, we must first be clear what that theory predicts. Evolutionary biology is no different. At first, this may seem like a hopeless task. Thanks to fossil and genetic evidence, we are beginning to sketch the evolutionary history of life on Earth, but we have almost no ability to predict specifically which genes will evolve in the future or what species will exist a million years from now. The evolutionary history of life on Earth is replete with random accidents that shaped its future: asteroid impacts, novel viruses, climatic changes, volcanic eruptions, lucky mutations, etc. If we ever find an exoplanet with an alien ecosystem, we do not know in advance what species we would find.

While our general theory of evolutionary biology does not predict that humans, specifically, must come into existence, it does make predictions about the process of evolution and the expected relationships between living and extinct species. Consider one of the most famous examples of predictions from the theory. Because unguided evolution can only make relatively modest changes as the eons pass, and we knew that fish predated land vertebrates, the constraints of evolution predicted that we would probably find fossils of an intermediate species—an early amphibian. Moreover, since we knew from prior fossil discoveries that amphibians likely developed between 360 million and 385 million years ago, the evolutionary ancestor of amphibians would likely be found in rock dating back to that period. In 2004, researchers Edward B. Daeschler, Neil Shubin, and Farish A. Jenkins Jr. set out on an expedition to the Canadian arctic where they knew they could find rocks that were 375–383 million years old.[12] There, they discovered fossils of Tiktaalik, a species halfway between fish and amphibians. The discovery of Tiktaalik was a striking demonstration of the predictive power of evolutionary biology.

---

[12] Shubin, Neil H., Edward B. Daeschler, and Farish A. Jenkins. *The pectoral fin of Tiktaalik roseae and the origin of the tetrapod limb.* Nature 440.7085 (2006): 764-771.

As we saw in the last section, we can expect all evolutionary processes to have a few things in common. Though we may not know which species we will find on an alien world, we expect to see the same traces of evolution on every evolved world.

Prediction 1: Descent

The first property of evolved worlds is descent. All individuals are reproductions of their parent or parents. Descent may take the form of cell division, egg laying, or live birth. Descent is necessary because, like our maze, adjacent environments can be deadly, and most species cannot perceive the danger directly. For example, a bacterium does not know that it has swum into a water droplet that will dry out in the daytime heat. A rabbit does not know that a fox regularly hunts in this hedgerow. A locust does not know that all the food for miles around has already been consumed by its brethren. If there were only one rabbit or only one locust, the process of life on Earth would end abruptly as soon as that individual ran into danger. So, each species must reproduce itself fast enough to escape predation, starvation, and disease. Each species must also have enough mutation or genetic variation to allow its population to adapt to changes in the environment and to spread to nearby environments.

Prediction 2: Common Descent

Because every species is the result of descent from its ancestors, every species on the same evolutionary tree has common ancestors stretching all the way back to the first life. On Earth, there is a single tree of life, as far as we know. Every species on Earth is related. Humans and bananas have a common ancestor.

Prediction 3: Common Composition

The human ability to design technology is powerful because our minds can understand how existing technology works in an abstract way, then reinvent that same technology to meet a new objective. Humans invented the wheel millennia ago. The first wheels were probably made of wood. But we understand that what is essential about the wheel is its rigidity and geometric structure. Consequently, we can easily design and build wheels out of metal or inflatable rubber tubing. Similarly, because we understand the function of automobile body panels and the properties of various materials, we can replace steel car bodies with aluminum, or aluminum with plastic.

In contrast, the process of evolution has no mind. When evolution invents a chemical mechanism through its process of random trial and natural selection, it has no mind with which to understand the abstract principles of its invention. Once evolution selects a choice of material or mechanism, it cannot easily replace that material or mechanism with an alternative.

Moreover, when evolution solves problems, it often does so by co-opting existing systems or by using the side effects of an existing system as the basis for something new. Consequently, many ancient biological mechanisms are frozen into the species that are living today. For example, almost all animals use adenosine triphosphate (ATP) as their energy-carrying molecule and employ mitochondria to convert sugar into ATP. Anatomically, animals as diverse as humans, cats, and pythons share similar features, such as skeletons, livers, hearts, and brains. Thus, evolution predicts that disparate species will share ancient biochemical mechanisms and anatomical features.

Prediction 4: Numerous Species

As we saw with our maze example, evolutionary development fills every available niche in the maze with life. In ecology, we see that almost every environment has single-celled life, multi-celled life, plants, grazers, predators, and scavengers. It is estimated that there are about two million species of life on Earth. Thus, we expect that evolved life on an alien planet would, if it were complex, consist of an ecosystem with a very large number of species.

Prediction 5: Long Timelines

Evolution is much faster than random guessing, but it still takes time for generations of life to breed and mutate. We expect complex life will take millions or billions of years to evolve on every planet.

Prediction 6: Survival as Sole Utility

Cars and airplanes cooperate with each other. Transportation vehicles are neither predators nor prey. Had humans not existed, planes, trains, and automobiles would not exist. They owe their existence to their usefulness to humans. Biology is quite different. Algae, viruses, and lions do not exist solely because they are useful to other species. They exist simply because they can breed and reproduce in their environment. They exist because they can survive.

In some interpretations of the story of Genesis, there was no death in the Garden of Eden. Animals existed not merely because they could. Lions had giant fangs not for ripping the flesh of wildebeest but for aesthetic purposes. The animals existed in harmony as companions for man. That is, the purpose of animal life in Eden was companionship and aesthetic beauty.

Evolution cares nothing for aesthetics and companionship unless they directly impact survival. While we find companionship in livestock and pets, our animals' ancestors did not evolve to produce companions for humans. Rather, a few species of animals have adapted to living with humans as a survival strategy. Cattle and chickens end up on our dinner table, but these species survive because we act to maintain their populations. Dogs create social relationships with humans that resemble their ancestors' social relationships as pack hunters.

We expect most evolved life on all worlds to exist in a state of conflict, of predator versus prey. A planet wherein all life cooperates is unlikely to be evolved.

Prediction 7: Knowledge Is Learned

Humans dominate Earth's environment because we augment our biological capability with learning. Moreover, knowledge advances much faster than biology, allowing humans to adapt to new conditions in less than a single generation. The fact that knowledge is learned from our environment might seem unremarkable, but until the recent invention of AI and machine learning, none of our human designs were capable of learning. Almost all our technology is preprogrammed at the factory. When you buy a television, it is preprogrammed for its specific task. If we discovered a species of reptile that understood particle accelerators or a species of octopus that understood general relativity, it would be excellent evidence that these species were designed and preprogrammed, because these species do not live in environments where they could possibly have learned that information.

In the story of Genesis, God creates a single human who understands the language and culture of God. This is analogous to a manufacturer shipping a robot that is not only able to learn, but is already preprogrammed with language, knowledge, and culture. In contrast, evolutionary processes in a purely material universe cannot accomplish such a feat as creating Adam. Evolution must first develop rudimentary biological cognition. Once knowledge is facilitated by biology, the shared knowledge and culture of individuals makes further enhancements in cognition advantageous. Evolution requires many generations and mutations for advanced learning and culture to develop in evolved species. And the culture and technology that develops is in response to the environment in which humans live. Albert Einstein devised his theory of general relativity only after humans developed telescopes and instrumentation.

This seventh prediction is closely related to the sixth. If a designer intends life to have a purpose other than mere survival, the designer will likely need to preprogram species to behave in a non-adversarial fashion.

Prediction 8: Vulnerability to Physics

Mythology tells stories of creatures that violate the laws of physics. For example, vampires cannot be harmed except by a stake through the heart or by exposure to sunlight. Angels are completely invulnerable to physical action, and there is nothing to prevent an angel from comfortably sitting at the core of a neutron star. Evolutionary biology acting on a chemical substrate is inherently limited. Being the result of chemical interactions, all evolved life forms are vulnerable to extremes of heat, acidity, radiation, pressure, and other physical forces. Evolution on a chemical substrate cannot create angels.

Alien Worlds

My list of predictions of evolution may not be exhaustive, but we can expect them to apply to all naturally evolved worlds. Alien worlds may be very different from our own. On worlds where gravity is very strong, perhaps life will exist as an ecology of flatworms. On rocky, Earth-like planets, perhaps evolution results in species that seem familiar to us, with taxa that resemble amphibians, reptiles, and mammals. But the specific solutions found by evolutionary processes do not matter much with respect to the eight predictions. If alien species use a genetic language distinct from DNA or RNA, we can expect their genomes to demonstrate the same patterns of common descent and common composition. We expect life on evolved alien worlds to be mostly adversarial, if sometimes symbiotic.

Of all these predictions, the one we might think easiest to vary is the prediction of numerous species. Consider a possible world on which life consists of a single, giant entity—say, a giant fungus covering an entire continent. Each tendril of the fungus learns from its local environment and passes on its knowledge to the other tendrils. Such a life form, if it could evolve, would violate our prediction that multiple species are required. However, for the fungus to learn from its environment, it needs to discover what doesn't work by trial and error. It needs to fail sometimes.

Perhaps our hypothetical fungus has rare genetic variation in its tendrils, and when a tendril dies, it does not affect the rest of its body. But when a tendril hits upon a new niche, it thrives and sends genetic messages to the rest of its body, so that whenever any other part of its body finds a similar niche, it will know how to create thriving tendrils. In terms of our maze analogy, it is as if all the life forms in the maze have formed a single union, with genetic "knowledge" spanning the entire maze.

Though it looks at first as if we have bypassed the prediction of numerous species, there are several problems with our hypothetical fungus. In effect, the tendrils have become species of their own. Though they may share genetic material spanning the entire continent, they must exclusively express genetic instructions corresponding to their own niche. The system resembles evolution with multiple species but with very high levels of horizontal gene transfer. That is, if we narrowly define an individual of a species as existing within its own skin, then it looks as if we are dealing with a single individual. Yet, the evolutionary algorithm requires both individuality and trial and error to play a role in development.

Another problem is that the grand entity is likely to splinter into adversarial life forms. A large mold would likely get broken into distinct pieces by natural disasters like floods, earthquakes, or volcanic activity. These severed pieces are likely to evolve away from one another while separated by physical barriers, and there is no guarantee that, should these pieces ever meet, they would see each other as kin. They might instead see each other as prey.

Since tendrils would need to operate semi-autonomously, they might suffer from the analog of cancer, with tendrils going rogue and feeding off the main body of the fungus. Should any such rebellion occur, it seems unlikely that it would result in multiple individuals breaking away from the whole. This would result in an ecosystem of tendrils that are no longer part of the grand collective, all competing for the same resources.

Finally, we should ask whether such a singular entity could arise in the first place. These hypothetical tendrils are a distributed and diverse collection of biological agents that share their genetic technology with neighboring tendrils, receiving useful genetic technology in exchange. That is, they are unconsciously playing a non-zero-sum game with the rest of the network. But in any such game, there is the possibility of defection. A tendril that learns to accept genetic technology from the body without contributing any of its own genetic innovation will perform better than the rest of the body. With the potential for defection ever present in evolutionary history, it is difficult to imagine that the resulting ecosystem will contain a single species or a single organism.

Thus, the eight predictions of evolutionary biology outlined in this chapter are general and can be expected to apply to all (or most) alien ecosystems.

Summary

Using maze traversal as an analogy for biological problem solving, we can see the differences between design, pure random guessing, and evolution. Design can find solutions nearly instantly, jumping straight to the solution without any intermediary. Randomly guessing a predetermined path through the maze fails to find a solution within the age of the universe for all but the simplest problems. Evolution finds maze solutions over millions of years, producing an ecosystem with millions of species.

Evolution has no goal and no forethought. Nature tries random variations within a population, and the surviving population serves as a memory of survival fitness. Intrinsic to the evolutionary algorithm are principles that lead to our eight predictions about evolved life. Though life on every evolved world may be very different, we expect all evolved life, all evolved natural history, to share observable properties.

4
Divine Design

> *"Man with all his shrewdness is as stupid*
> *about understanding by himself*
> *the mysteries of God, as an ass is incapable of*
> *understanding musical harmony."*
>
> — *John Calvin*

Our analysis of evolutionary biology in the last chapter makes clear that the theory is highly predictive of what we observe. Had evolutionary mechanisms not been responsible for life, our scientific investigations could easily have refuted the theory. We now turn our attention to divine design and ask, what does design predict? Nothing.

An all-powerful, infinitely intelligent creator can create whatever it wants. There is no way to say in advance what such a being would do. God is totally unconstrained. Divine design predicts nothing and everything, rendering it the worst possible theory. Alas, human psychology makes this flaw difficult to see.

A good explanation predicts what it explains. Sir Isaac Newton's gravity explained the motion of objects falling to Earth and the motions of planets orbiting the Sun because it predicts them. Karl Popper, the great philosopher of science, would say that Newton's gravity was a good theory because it forbids alternative outcomes. In Newton's theory, rocks cannot float up into the sky, and Venus cannot simply wander off into deep space.

Evolutionary biology is explanatory because it is predictive. Evolutionary process involves random inputs, so we cannot predict everything. We could not have predicted we would find the platypus, for example. But as discussed in the last chapter, evolutionary biology is highly predictive. Evolution forbids violations of those predictions, and so finding violations of, say, the prediction of common descent would refute evolutionary theory.

God, however, does not explain anything because the theory does not predict anything. This is not obvious. When we think of God acting in the world, our tendency is to first assume that God exists and then ask if there is any possible way God could perform the act and if there is any possible purpose God could have in so acting. And because God is infinitely powerful and infinitely wily, there always is a possible way God could act in that way. People like to say that God acts in mysterious ways. What they mean is that their theory of God makes no predictions. The answer to the question, "Why did this happen?" is simply the answer, "God wanted it that way for mysterious reasons, and he has the power to make it happen."

The generic theory of divine design predicts nothing and prohibits nothing. It is because of this lack of explanatory power that intelligent design has failed to persuade scientists and educators of its intellectual merit. Let's take a brief look at the history of the intelligent design movement in the United States.

The Intelligent Design Movement

In 2004, the Dover Area School District of York County, Pennsylvania, mandated that high school students be taught not only evolutionary biology but also a theory of intelligent design. Advocates for adding intelligent design to the syllabus portrayed their movement as secular and scientific, saying nothing about who or what they believed was responsible for designing living systems. For its part, the scientific community argued that the intelligent design movement was a religious creationist movement and pseudoscience. In 2005, when the dispute over the syllabus was resolved in federal court, Judge John E. Jones III ruled that intelligent design was indeed creationism, and that its teaching in public schools violated the First Amendment's prohibition on the establishment of religion.

Intelligent design failed as a science because it made no predictions of its own. Instead, it simply critiqued gaps in our understanding of evolutionary biology. The leading lights of the movement attempted to define criteria that could be used to identify biological mechanisms that were designed rather than evolved. In principle, this was a reasonable strategy. In practice, the effort ultimately failed.

The most famous design criterion was *irreducible complexity*, devised by American biochemist Michael Behe.[13] A system is said to be irreducibly complex if it consists of multiple components, and the removal of any single component destroys the function of the whole. Behe argued that if a complex system has multiple parts and none of the parts serve any function on their own, then evolution has no incentive to invent the components individually. For such a complex system to emerge, Behe claimed that evolution would need an extraordinarily improbable coincidence—multiple simultaneous mutations that work together in a novel and useful way. Behe argued that the probability of these coincidences is so small that such complex systems must have been designed. Returning to our maze analogy, Behe's argument was that some mazes are structured in such a way that evolution would have to take an improbable series of blind guesses to navigate the maze.

Irreducibly complex systems do exist in nature. The problem with Behe's thesis lies in his claim that evolution cannot create them. To build an irreducibly complex system, evolution need not invent all the parts

---

[13] Behe, M.J. *Darwin's Black Box: The Biochemical Challenge of Evolution.* Touchstone, New York, 1998.

simultaneously. Evolution typically reuses proteins or gene sequences that evolved in one context, modifying them for use in another. Suppose that within individuals of a species, biology synthesizes two proteins, A and B. Each protein, on its own, helps the species to survive. Suppose that, later, a mutation occurs such that the organism produces both the original protein, A, and a new protein, α. Protein α has lost its original function and is useless on its own, but by good fortune, the combination of α and B has a new and useful side effect. The two proteins form an interacting complex, $C = \alpha + B$, which helps the species survive even better than before. Now, suppose that in later generations, a mutation causes the species to synthesize protein β as well as B. As before, protein β has lost its original solitary function, but protein β creates a newer and better version of C. That is, $C' = \alpha + \beta$ is better than the original complex $\alpha + B$. C' is now irreducibly complex. Neither α nor β has any use on its own, and removing either of them would stop the complex from working.

Thus, Behe's argument that evolution cannot possibly create irreducibly complex systems does not stand up to critique. Nonetheless, to this day, advocates of intelligent design still quote Behe's argument. Whereas scientists engage with their community and accept the scientific reasoning of their peers, promoters of intelligent design theory simply refuse to engage with the scientific response to their doctrine.

With no knockdown argument and no testable predictions, the intelligent design movement's critique of evolution was reduced to complaints about gaps in our understanding of the details of evolutionary history. Here again, gaps arguments can work. But knowing how and when they work makes all the difference.

God of the Gaps

You may have heard the phrase "God of the Gaps," which is employed as a derogatory term for the invocation of God to explain gaps in our current scientific understanding of the natural world. Historically, the gaps keep getting smaller, and the God of the Gaps shrinks along with them. As a rule, relying on God to fill in gaps in our understanding of the world does not work.

As we saw in Chapter 2, not all gaps threaten a theory. A gap is only a problem when we expect to see evidence or when we lack evidence entirely. As we saw in the last chapter, evolution makes many narrow predictions that are plainly consistent with the evidence. Simultaneously, we expect evolutionary biology to have gaps in its fossil record and in our natural history of biochemical mechanisms.

Gaps in evolutionary biology are like the gaps in Bob's prosecutor's case in Chapter 2. Fossilization is an extremely rare process. To become fossilized, an animal must perish in an environment where its flesh and bones won't be carried off by scavengers or broken down by bacteria or erosion. To be discovered by humans, erosion must remove just enough rock to expose the fossil in a way that investigators will find it. Far less than 1% of all species that ever lived will be preserved in fossils for humans to discover. There are about 11,000 species of birds living today, but only about a thousand species of dinosaur have been identified from fossils, even though dinosaurs lived on Earth for 170 million years.

However, there are enough accessible fossils that, even in Darwin's time, naturalists could piece together the general pattern of Earth's natural history. Evidence discovered over the last century and a half makes this pattern much clearer. Had evolution been a false theory, that evidence need not have lined up at all. When the famous biologist J.B.S. Haldane was asked what evidence would falsify evolution, he is alleged to have answered, "Rabbits in the pre-Cambrian," referring to the hypothetical appearance of recent mammals before even vertebrate fish had evolved. It is true that there are intermediate species that evolution predicts but which fossil hunters have yet to uncover, but this does not weaken the argument, because we expect to be missing more than 99% of all species from the fossil record.

Advocates for intelligent design claim that evolutionary theory has failed to explain biology because we do not yet know exactly how certain biochemical mechanisms evolved. For example, the flagellum, a sophisticated rotary propulsion system that is found in some species of bacteria, is irreducibly complex, and we do not know its evolutionary history. However, this gap is only harmful to the theory if it can be proven that evolution could not explain it in principle or if evolutionary theory predicts that we ought to have discovered this biochemical history by now. As explained earlier, evolution can create irreducibly complex systems, so the evolution skeptic can make no hay out of such a gap. Moreover, since the biochemistry of bacteria from a billion years ago has long since been washed away, it comes as no surprise that we do not know which molecular precursors were repurposed when the flagellum was evolved.

Advocates of intelligent design, unable to show that evolution is impossible, must instead show that their theory is a better explanation. To do this, they must explain why the world we see is more probable under their theory than under the theory that no intelligence was involved.

Design's Predictions

In principle, a theory of design can be quite predictive. There are many phenomena that we casually and reasonably interpret as the result of human design. Graffiti, cakes, music, pocket watches, and jet airplanes are easily recognizable examples. Design is a viable theory in these cases, not least because we know that human designers exist. We understand not only that there are designers in our environment, but also their means, motive, and opportunity. We understand the utility of their creations because these creators are finite and needy.

Consider the pocket watch. Pocket watches are useful to people who need to arrive at appointments on time, cook dishes for consistent lengths of time, or study physics. If we landed on an alien world and found a pocket watch on the ground, we would predict the existence of an intelligent designer who needed to synchronize events or measure time intervals. In fact, by looking at the precision of the mechanism and the dial, we could tell how precisely the designer needed to measure time intervals. By looking at the materials used in its construction, we may also learn what types of technology the designer was capable of assembling.

Although we sometimes create things exclusively for their aesthetic value, this is not true of most of our inventions. We create many more soda cans than oil paintings. Finding something that appears designed enables us to predict not only that there is a designer but that there are likely many more designed things floating around that the same designer would find useful. Moreover, if the pocket watch we discover is only a centimeter in diameter, it probably belongs to a designer with correspondingly small hands (and pockets).

When humans design complex systems, such as software or jet planes, we need to do so in such a way that we can wrap our minds around the construction and maintenance of our creations. This means making modular systems where a failure in one module doesn't cause a myriad of failures in unrelated modules. It means making designs as logical and simple as possible. Finally, whatever we design must be delivered in time to serve our needs. We will not spend 500 years building a tunnel under a river when we can build a bridge in five years instead.

Clearly, the complexity of life does not appear designed by finite creatures like humans or by advanced alien civilizations. Life on Earth took 3.8 billion years to evolve. What use is Earth's life to a finite species if it takes billions of years to deliver its product?

Though we can imagine seeding a world with life so that we could harvest its plants and animals for food, such an endeavor would only be worthwhile if it were competitive with farming our existing crops and animals. The latter would take decades at most.

If intelligent life is the goal, why evolve life on a planet for billions of years when we can build an artificial intelligence instead?

If the designers of life on Earth were finite like us, they would likely seed the Earth with existing life that could develop rapidly. We would not expect to see a tree of life, but just a few leaves of such a tree. This is not what we see in Earth's natural history. If life on Earth is designed, it must be designed by a mind for whom billions of years is the blink of an eye and for whom competing technologies are irrelevant.

Infinite Designers

Intelligent design advocates were often cagey about the identity of the designer, but it was obvious that they believed the designer in question was God. If he exists, God is infinitely powerful and has an infinitely creative intellect, so it would certainly be possible for God to create the kind of life we observe on Earth in the allotted time. Yet, it is not obvious that an infinitely powerful designer like God could possibly exist in a metaphysical sense. God's infinite powers seem like they are the inventions of a child—a child with no theory of epistemology and a simple desire to make God all-powerful. For example, when God makes perfect predictions about actual and hypothetical events, does God simulate all the alternatives? And, if he does, would that not instantiate those alternative worlds as simulations?

Indeed, questions about theistic simulation are relevant to the theory of theistic evolution. If God arranged the particles and fields in the early universe knowing that the result would be the formation of Earth and the evolution of humans, did God automatically know how to do this, did God compute all the alternatives and thereby create other worlds, or none of the above? More generally, how does God's knowledge work?

To me, these questions throw into doubt the entire conception of an omniscient deity. However, as this is not a book about metaphysics, I shall set aside the metaphysical question of whether God can exist and proceed under the provisional assumption that God is a metaphysical possibility.

Religious thinkers like to infer God's motives for creating our biosphere from their interpretations of religious texts. Scientists and rationalists find religious texts to be unpersuasive because there is no compelling reason to believe these texts are anything more than the speculations of humans from ages past. But even if we take theological speculation seriously, God's motives are still not predictive. Most theists are unwilling to say what God's purpose was in creating life on Earth in the way that he allegedly did so. Consequently, such theories of intelligent design make no predictions of their own. As we have seen, if no narrow predictions are made, there is no way to raise a theory's posterior probability with new evidence.

Without the ability to make predictions, theists work in reverse. Instead of predicting in advance what God would do, they simply look at the world with the prior assumption that God designed it. Of course, if there are no predictions, one world is no more or less likely than any other.

It is no less likely that God would create life of the type we see on Earth than any other. This seemingly innocuous statement is, it turns out, the undoing of theistic design as a hypothesis. If I have a trillion-sided die, rolling a one on that die is no less likely than rolling any other number. The key insight here is that evolved life of the type we see on Earth is an infinitesimal sliver of the possible life-bearing worlds that an all-powerful designer could create.

Let's compare the predictions of evolutionary biology with the alternative possibilities that an omnipotent designer possesses. As we shall see, thinking creatively about what a designer could do shows us why design is such a dismal failure. In the following analysis, the term "designer" refers to an omnipotent, omniscient designer.

Evolutionary Prediction 1: Descent

Evolved life forms require built-in reproductive capabilities. But human inventions do not. Indeed, no automobile has ever given birth to another automobile. Nor would we want it to. Humans either create bespoke artifacts or manufacture them in factories. Just like humans, a designer has no need for species at all. A designer could create every living thing as a bespoke, custom creation, sharing no biology with any other. Moreover, none of these creations need to have any built-in reproductive capability. Of course, a designer *could* create reproductive biology if they wanted to, but it is optional. On a planet of two million species, a designer has the choice to make each one either bespoke/manufactured or self-replicating. There are $2^{2,000,000}$ permutations of this choice. Thus, merely by observing that all the millions of species of life on Earth propagate by descent, we have potent evidence against design.

Evolutionary Prediction 2: Common Descent

Evolution predicts that humans will share DNA with chimpanzees, cats, and even bananas. Indeed, it appears that we share about 98% of our DNA with chimps, 90% with cats, and 60% with bananas. This is not predicted by design. Many creationists and intelligent design advocates claim that evolutionary mechanisms can explain variation within species but deny that evolution can explain the differences between species. For example, they claim that evolution can explain how house cats and chihuahuas are related to their wild predator cousins, but evolution cannot explain how a dog and a cat are related, or how a cat and a human are related. Into this gap they insert God as a candidate explanation. God wanted humans, cats, and dogs, so he created humans, cats, and dogs independently. Again, it is perfectly within the capabilities of an omnipotent God to perform such a feat. But if God does this, there is no reason why humans, cats, and dogs should share any DNA whatsoever. It's not easier for God to reuse DNA. When one is infinitely powerful, nothing is easier or more difficult than anything else. When we mapped the genomes of humans, cats, and dogs, we might have discovered that the species share no DNA in common. Instead of finding two million variations of the same genome, we might have encountered two million thoroughly unique genomes.

Conservatively, biologists have sequenced the genomes of 500 species, and no evidence of bespoke genome design has been found. Yet, had life been designed, each species might have either evolved or been a unique, bespoke creation. There are at least $2^{2,000,000}$ choices a designer could make that evolution cannot, and 2^{500} of these have been tested.

These incredible odds of $2^{2,000,000}$ do not even include the number of possible genomes that a designer could implement. How many options does a designer have in crafting a bespoke genome? Presumably, there is a vast number of completely custom genomes that a designer could create. In the science fiction film, *The Fifth Element*, the supreme being has an engineered genome that is 300 times more complex than that of a human. Presumably, God could improve on such engineering in an infinite number of ways.

Evolutionary Prediction 3: Common Composition

A designer is not subject to the compositional limitations of evolutionary biology. There is nothing to prevent a designer from creating plastic turtles, nuclear-powered antelopes, or sheep with wire wool. Again, if the designer were merely taking Earth's existing species and tweaking them with different materials, another permutation factor of $2^{2,000,000}$ would be inadequate to describe the available options.

Evolutionary Prediction 4: Numerous Species

There is nothing preventing a designer from populating a planet exclusively with rabbits. Since the designer has access to infinite energy, these rabbits could be powered by divine energy with no need for grass or plants to consume. Evolution has no such option. Not only is there no such thing as divine energy in the naturalistic evolutionary picture, but there is also no way for evolution to go from single-celled life to rabbits without creating millions of intermediate forms.

A designer can also populate a planet with bespoke individuals. There are perhaps a trillion individual life forms on Earth. These individuals fall into two million species, but a designer could create every individual uniquely. This would be like having a million times as many species. On an Earth-like planet, a designer can create about a million (10^6) additional permutations of the number of species.

Evolutionary Prediction 5: Millions of Years

In Genesis, God creates the entire universe in six days and all life in one day. Many theologians are liberal in their interpretation of these primordial days. Some say that such a day could have been millions of years. But it would be no less within God's power to create the world in the blink of an eye. Evolution, of course, has no such option. If evidence showed that Earth's natural history had really occurred over a mere 6,000 years, there would be no way evolution could explain it unless evolutionary biology operated a million times faster than has been observed.

Evolutionary Prediction 6: Survival as Utility

Interpretations of Genesis are diverse. One interpretation is that God created life in the Garden of Eden for aesthetic purposes. This means that the lion's teeth were not for ripping apart flesh, but just for looks. Life in the Garden was collaborative, not competitive. This is *not* the kind of life that evolution can create. I do not cite Genesis as a straw-man version of theistic design, but as an example of the kind of theory that people entertained before they knew about evolutionary biology. Of course God could make Eden!

Imagine a world created to serve as a manufacturing facility. Raw materials drop down from above, and the alien inhabitants take the raw materials and produce some final product, whether that be art or electronics. These final products then ascend to the heavens. The life forms on this planet, having been designed to serve as manufacturers, are completely cooperative. Such an alien factory planet could not evolve, for two reasons. First, there is no way for evolution to know in advance what needs to be manufactured, and therefore no way for random mutations to incrementally advance toward the goal of the factory. If the factory will make televisions, how do protobacteria know what a television is, and how do the protobacteria get a greater payout for evolving toward a species that can build a TV than it gets for simply outcompeting its neighbors for nutrients?

Moreover, it seems that there is no limit to the number of utilities or values an infinite agent might possess. Contemporary humans value all sorts of cultural sophistication, from fine coffee to comic irony to mumblecore movies. Our values, tastes, and purposes are becoming more and more diverse as our culture develops. Does an infinite designer not have an infinite number of possible tastes beyond mere survival?

Thus, the number of possible utilities for life seems infinitely greater in the case of design.

Evolutionary Prediction 7: Knowledge Is Learned

In fiction, we imagine animals with sophisticated minds, culture, and language. The serpent of Genesis, the Cheshire Cat, or Bayard the horse from French medieval myth. There is nothing to prevent a designer from creating life forms with both cognition and culture all at once. Presumably, the serpent of Genesis always knew how to speak.

So, had the species of Earth been designed, there is no reason why, say, bears could not be experts on astronomy while orangutans are the planet's greatest authority on hydrodynamics. Just as humans design and build electronic calculators, it would be easy for a designer to create species with knowledge built into them without the need for evolved cognition or learning.

Here again, design presents us with an infinite number of possible creative variations of life on Earth that are out of the reach of evolutionary biology.

Evolutionary Prediction 8: Vulnerability to Physics

Design theism can make entities that have structure beyond chemistry. The Bible speaks of angels as spiritual beings that are invulnerable to physics. In contrast, evolution on a chemical substrate cannot create such beings. Evolution is dependent on the chemistry of the world for its construction and raw materials. How many variations of Earth's phyla can we dream up that feature different invulnerable creatures? The list may be infinite.

Infinite Permutations

Evolutionary processes acting on chemical substrates are far more restrictive than divine design. Any theologian who claims otherwise is being disingenuous. In the preceding analysis, I outlined a vast number of possible designed ecospheres that are variations of Earth's one evolved world. For every evolved Earth-like world, there are at least $2^{4,000,500}$ design alternatives, and probably an infinite number. This immediately suggests that the *a priori* likelihood that a designer would use evolution to construct humans is very nearly zero.

In my experience, the first question theists ask in response to this argument is, "Who's to say that God would not create a world that looks exactly like the one we see?"

Of course, no one is saying it is not possible for God to create the world we see. If God intended such a world, it would be trivial for him to create it. But the Counterargument from Design is an argument about probability, not possibility. If we assume nothing about the designer, there is no more reason for the designer to create an evolved world than one of the infinity of alternatives.

Theists may then follow up with the question, "Isn't it arrogant to say God would not construct us using evolutionary processes?" Not at all. Suppose all we knew was that God created life on a planet, but we did not know what kinds of creatures existed there. Because we have not yet looked at the planet's biology or natural history, we can only imagine what the world would look like. We would literally have no idea what to expect.

Indeed, when the authors of Genesis envisaged God's creation, they broke every prediction of evolutionary biology except for the multitude of species (which they could easily have noticed by looking around them).

In the millennia since Genesis was written, fantasy and science fiction authors have imagined an assortment of magical worlds that violate the predictions of evolution acting on chemical substrates. It seems absurd to suggest that the creativity of human authors or the sophistication of human civilization is more than an infinitesimal sliver of an infinite creative force.

What would be arrogant is to claim that God would not create these other sorts of worlds. It is not I who is arrogantly claiming to know what God would create. I am quite specifically disclaiming any knowledge of how God would create any specific world. For this reason, every possible world God could create gets a little bit of the prior probability, just as every side of a trillion-sided die gets a little bit of the prior probability.

In contrast, naturalism will always create worlds that appear evolved. If I have a one-sided die (or a trillion-sided die with a one on every face) and a trillion-sided die (with sides numbered one to a trillion) and randomly roll one of the dice, and it comes up one, you know it was the one-sided die that was selected.

Promissory Explanations

Suppose that, to everyone's surprise, the daytime sky changes from blue to purple. I step forward and declare, "I have an explanation! Science explains how the sky changed from blue to purple!"

"Excellent," says the crowd. "Do go on!"

"No, that's it," says I. "I mean that we have not solved all the scientific mysteries of the universe, and as Arthur C. Clarke famously said, sufficiently advanced technology is indistinguishable from magic. So, science can explain why the sky has changed color."

Although there would no doubt be many people who believe a scientific explanation for the effect could one day be found, I believe there are few who would concur that science had explained (past tense) the phenomenon. I have not explained with science but merely promised that a scientific explanation will one day be discovered.

Similarly, when people assert that design explains the world we observe, they are giving a promissory explanation. Design does not explain the world as we find it. If it could explain it, it would also predict it. But proponents of divine design can make no predictions.

This means that there is a critical asymmetry between evolution and design as theories for explaining life. Whereas evolution is a predictive, mechanical theory, design merely promises a future explanation. If we understood the mind of God well enough to predict his rationales, to predict why evolution is better than the infinity of alternatives, then we could predict evolutionary processes above the design alternatives. Indeed, if our theory of divine design could predict specific species, it would be even better than evolutionary biology. Alas, we have no such theory of design, and no reason to increase the share of the design prior that looks like natural processes.

5

The Counterargument from Design

"Bayesian statistics is difficult in the sense that thinking is difficult."

— Donald Arthur Berry

We are now equipped to state the Counterargument from Design in more formal terms. The general argument runs as follows:

Premise 1: If naturalism is true, we expect all (or most) complex life to be evolved.

Premise 2: If divine design is true, it is extremely probable that life will appear designed, because there are far more ways (and possibly infinitely more ways) that life can appear designed than evolved.

Premise 3: All things being equal, we should expect to find ourselves on a world that is typical in the space of possible worlds.

Premise 4: If life were designed, that space of possibilities would consist almost entirely of worlds that do not look evolved. If life were evolved unguided, that space would consist almost entirely of worlds that look evolved.

Premise 5: Life appears to have evolved.

Conclusion: Naturalistic evolution is far more probable than divine design.

To be more precise, we can write the argument in probabilistic terms. Let's start our journey out with equal priors for naturalism and design:

$$P(N) = P(D) = 50\%$$

Because evolution is the only plausible mechanism by which blind physical processes can create the complex mechanisms within living things, we must conclude that any life we find in a naturalistic universe is going to look evolved. That is, the likelihood of finding that life appears evolved (E) given naturalism is approximately 100%:

$$P(E|N) \cong 1$$

The Counterargument from Design

Meanwhile, for every world that looks designed, designers can create an infinity of alternative worlds that appear designed by violating the eight predictions of evolutionary biology. This implies that evolved life is an infinitesimal subset of the predictions of design. I will call this very small number ϵ:

$$P(E|D) = \epsilon$$

Consequently, the probability that life is a product of design given that we find life to appear evolved is:

$$P(D|E) = \frac{P(D)P(E|D)}{P(D)P(E|D) + P(N)P(E|N)}$$

Since we start with equal prior probabilities, the priors cancel out, and we are left with a ratio of likelihoods:

$$P(D|E) = \frac{P(E|D)}{P(E|D) + P(E|N)}$$

$$\cong \frac{\epsilon}{\epsilon + 1}$$

Given that ϵ is extremely small, we can simplify the formula to

$$P(D|E) \cong \epsilon$$

That is, the probability that life on Earth was designed is approximately the ratio of the number of possible ways a designer could create a world that looks evolved divided by the number of possible ways a designer could create a world that looks obviously designed.

In visual terms, the Counterargument from Design looks like this:

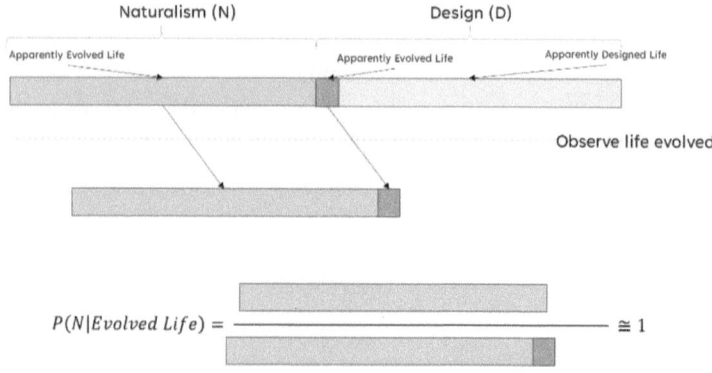

The parameter, ϵ, represents the fraction of the design half of the prior which is expected to appear evolved.

Let's answer two immediate objections which may be raised.

- In 1850, most people would have judged naturalism to be improbable. How can we justify equal prior probabilities in our argument?
- Naturalism, as understood today, has been fine-tuned and matched up with our observations of the world. Can we not do the same for theistic design? Can we not match up the modern neo-Darwinian synthesis against a revised vision of theistic design in which God intends an evolved world?

The philosophy of naturalism has existed since at least the time of Ancient Greek philosophers. Under naturalism, the universe operates on fixed, mechanical, nonmental laws. Under naturalism, abstractions may be real, causal, and explanatory, but they are implemented by the brain's physical machinery. Defined in this way, naturalism stands for a class of theories whose implications have yet to be fully understood.

Given a general theory like naturalism, we narrow down our conception of naturalism in response to the surprising things we learn about the world. These surprises may be the result of empirical laboratory experiments or from unexpected theoretical implications. For an experimental example, naturalists of the early 20th century were surprised by the astronomical observation that the Milky Way is not the entire universe but is instead only one of trillions of galaxies. In the realm of theory, naturalists were surprised when Darwin showed that the then-understood principles of population biology would result in evolution of species. As Strevens puts it in his *Notes on Bayesian Confirmation Theory*, we are not logically omniscient beings, so even if we know the core principles of a theory, we do not automatically know the implications. The implications must be worked out using logic, simulation, or other methods, and some of those implications will surprise us.

Darwin's theory of evolution by natural selection was a discovery about the theoretical implications of population, reproduction, and selection. Before Darwin wrote *On the Origin of Species*, it was already known that species have populations, reproduce with some heredity, and are selected by the environment and each other. What was surprising was that the statistics of natural selection could explain the evolution of life.

Thus, even though design was the best explanation of life before Darwin, we do not have to set the prior probability that life arose through natural means to some tiny value. The thinkers of the early 19th century did not know that naturalism implicitly implied the evolutionary pattern we had observed.

We can also see why there is an asymmetry between naturalism and theism. There is nothing in theism that tells us that it is necessary for God to design a world that looks evolved. Indeed, the authors of Genesis imagined something very different. Since there is no theoretical implication from God to evolution, there is no license to narrow the design theory to predict evolution without also narrowing the corresponding prior.

Perhaps, if we understood the world of the divine, if we understood the choices that all gods are compelled to make, we might somehow show that most divine creators will create evolved worlds. Alas, not only has this not been done, but it also seems rather implausible we could ever think like an omniscient, omnipotent god, and thereby conclude that designers must create a naturally evolved world.

6

Objections

"He has a right to criticize, who has a heart to help."

— *Abraham Lincoln*

The Counterargument from Design is profoundly counterintuitive. When I first shared an outline of the argument with my friends, I received considerable pushback even from my atheist colleagues: *If God can easily create the world we see, how can this argument be correct?*

For my part, the argument seemed straightforward, and so I was surprised that my friends had such a negative reaction to the argument. I was even more surprised that I could find no formal version of this argument in journals or in popular culture. To put this in perspective, one of the most discussed theological arguments today is the Fine-Tuning

Argument. The Fine-Tuning Argument reasons from apparent coincidences in physics and cosmology to the existence of a designer who aligned the physical laws to create a life-bearing universe. The Fine-Tuning Argument and the Counterargument from Design are similar kinds of arguments, and I will compare them in detail in Chapter 7. If fine-tuning is a popular argument, why has no one formalized an argument from evolution?

My best explanation for the neglect of this argument has to do with psychology and epistemology. The default way that we reason is by narrative. If we can think of a possible story in which an agent takes an action, we irrationally make the leap to thinking that the intentional action is not only possible but probable. This is part of the reason why we love conspiracy theories. It is easy to imagine a powerful group of people who intend things to work out as they do and take whatever steps are necessary to make it happen as it does. Indeed, the theory that God designed a world that looked evolved is a conspiracy theory of sorts.

But the key reason that I arrived at the argument is that I have tried to cultivate Bayesian epistemology within my thinking. If I rationally believe something to be true in light of the evidence, there must be a Bayesian argument that supports my inference. Since I found the evidence for evolution compelling and I intuited that stereotypical design was ruled out by the evidence, I reasoned that it must be possible to construct a Bayesian argument to this effect.

Out of this rare perspective, the Counterargument from Design was born. Specifically, Bayes' Theorem led me to consider the likelihood that a designer would create a world that appeared evolved, and this in turn forced me to ask what alternatives the designer had. When I started on my analysis, I expected the argument to conclude that unguided evolution was somewhat more likely than design to explain life, but I was surprised to discover the most powerful argument for atheism I have ever seen.

Though the formal argument I present may be new, the intuition that evolution does more than just neutralize the design argument for God is not. Many people intuit that theism doesn't make a lot of sense in the light of evolution. In this sense, the Counterargument from Design is not a wholly new argument for atheism. Nonetheless, its potency will trigger a lot of skeptical responses, and I want to address these as best I can.

Every argument is based on assumptions, however general they may be, and critics of the argument are most likely to attack these first.

Non-Overlapping Magisteria

Paleontologist Stephen J. Gould famously argued that science and religion study two non-overlapping domains. According to Gould, science studies the world of fact, while religion studies the world of value, meaning, and purpose. Adherents to this view would hold that religion has no business making pronouncements about physical laws, and science has nothing to say about what we should value. That is, science may inform us about the world and may accurately describe the process by which humans make value judgments, but it cannot say anything intrinsic about how we ought to align our values. At best, science can tell us that if we value X, we ought to value Y.

Though Gould defined his non-overlapping magisteria quite narrowly, I will use the term a little more broadly. It is often said that science studies the physical, while religion and philosophy study the metaphysical. Indeed, metaphysical claims are often so far abstracted from reality that they cannot be tested experimentally. Consider the metaphysical theory of idealism. Idealism holds that reality is fundamentally mental and the world is a construct of mind. There are many theories of idealism, some containing a single mind, some containing many. We never perceive things in themselves. We only ever perceive mental representations of things. What if there are no things, just representations?

Naively, such a theory of idealism seems untestable. After all, whatever the experimental outcome, the result will be just another thing appearing to our conscious mind.

Most philosophers and scientists tend to want to stay in their respective lane. They adopt a general principle that physical experiments cannot tell us about metaphysical reality. This rule is also a little self-serving. Scientists get to teach evolutionary biology in schools, while priests get to pretend that science hasn't put them out of business.

Can we apply the principle of non-overlapping magisteria to the Counterargument for Design?

At first, it may seem that way. Here we have an argument that uses the scientific fact of our evolutionary history and concludes that a certain class of gods does not exist. With the same stroke, the Counterargument from

Design also neutralizes the value, meaning, and purpose of any religion that derives such things from the designer's existence.

However, the justification for non-overlapping magisteria is fuzzy at best. One of the most popular arguments for the existence of God is the Fine-Tuning Argument. This argument concludes that God exists because the odds of a universe being compatible with life is too improbable without divine intervention. The Fine-Tuning Argument is clearly arguing from physical law to the existence of a metaphysical designer. This seems quite an overlap. If the Fine-Tuning Argument is acceptable, then surely the Counterargument from Design is, too.

Moreover, metaphysical claims are rarely as remote from experimental testing as they might seem. Let's return to philosophical idealism. If everything is mental, why are brains entwined with physicality? Why do I know only what my physical brain can know rather than everything? Why do I have my perspective instead of yours? Why can brain surgery alter mental faculties, but mental activity cannot directly enact brain surgery? If minds are fundamental, why do we need physical brains to think with?

I am not a philosophical idealist, because a world in which physics is fundamental *requires* that physical brains be responsible for cognition, just as we observe. A world wherein the mental is fundamental does not have any of the same requirements or constraints. In many ways, the arguments against idealism and the dualism of body and soul are similarly Bayesian. In a purely physical world, things *must* be a certain way. In worlds where mentality is fundamental, many things don't have to be the way we have observed them to be.

God Must Exist

If God exists, he is very well-hidden. We are all atheistic about the God who makes his presence obvious to human eyes. But what if we could prove that a creator God must exist, whether or not we can find any physical evidence?

If God must necessarily exist, then probability becomes irrelevant. Many of the classical and medieval arguments for God's existence attempted to prove exactly this. If God were truly a necessary, creative feature of reality, then God must exist, even if we cannot see God directly. In Western philosophy, arguments for eternal, divine entities go back at least 2,500 years to the time of the Ancient Greek philosophers Pythagoras, Parmenides of Elea, Socrates, Plato, and Aristotle. Later, Thomas Aquinas, the medieval philosopher whose work forms the backbone of Catholic doctrine, constructed arguments not only for God's existence, but also for God's singular, personal, and moral nature. If the arguments of Aquinas are sufficiently robust, then probabilistic arguments from evidence don't matter. Divine intent would be woven into the fabric of all reality, and human morality would be connected to the creator.

A full exposition and critique of these classical arguments for God's existence is far beyond the scope of this book, but suffice it to say, most contemporary philosophers no longer find these arguments compelling. Each classical argument that God must exist has some critical flaw.

For example, the Cosmological Argument claims that if we are to avoid an infinite regress of causes without resorting to brute facts, then the universe must have been created by a "necessary" being (a first cause), and names God as this necessary being. However, as philosophy advanced, the discipline became more careful with language and logic. There is no such thing as necessity without context—if something is necessary, it must be necessary *for* something else. Yet, in this argument, God is necessary only to avoid the brute fact of the universe's existence. And God is just as much a brute fact as the universe itself, and no less complex.

The Impossibility of Evolution

Some will object to the Counterargument from Design on the grounds that they believe evolution is impossible. Some theologians have argued that unguided evolution is impossible in principle. Impossibility arguments stem from misunderstandings of the evolutionary process, but I feel they are popular enough that I should address them here.

Thermodynamics

One common argument against evolution is the claim that the evolutionary process violates the second law of thermodynamics, which states that in any closed system, entropy always increases. In physics, entropy has a rather specific physical and statistical definition. The entropy of a system is the number of microscopic states consistent with the macroscopic parameters of the system.

For example, given a box containing a fixed number of gas molecules and a fixed total energy and momentum, there are many ways that the energy, momentum, and position of the particles could be distributed. Some molecules will be moving faster than others, and there might be a few more molecules on one side of the container than the other, but the statistical distribution of locations and speeds will form a normal distribution. In a typical container of gas, most of the molecules will be moving quite fast, and the molecules will be distributed randomly throughout the container. But it is possible that the gas molecules could, by chance, end up in an unusually ordered configuration. For example, just by chance, all the molecules could end up on the left side of the container, while the right side is empty. Or we might find that, at one instant, all the gas molecules are stationary except for two very energetic molecules moving in opposite directions. This latter scenario resembles a billiard table with a fast zooming pair of cue balls and a stationary, unbroken rack of balls somewhere on the table. Such a scenario is unlikely to remain so pristine. If a cue ball hits the stationary balls, they will scatter and continue to scatter off one another. Though it is theoretically possible that the balls could return to their original racked state, there are many more unracked states they are more likely to be in.

The theory of statistical mechanics tells us that even if the laws of physics are microscopically reversible, the physics of large numbers of particles is statistically irreversible. The broken rack of balls is statistically unlikely to reassemble itself into a stationary, closely packed, and ordered arrangement.

The second law of thermodynamics explains why disorder arises from order in many physical situations. Of course, there are situations in which order seems to arise out of disorder. When crystals form in a pool of liquid or plants create flowers from soil, we seem to be getting ordered structure from disorder. However, this order emerging from disorder does not violate the second law. When order arises in crystal formation, there is a net increase in disorder. This happens because the increase in order in the crystal is offset by a corresponding increase in disorder in the environment. After the crystal forms, there are more ways to distribute evaporated water molecules in the surrounding atmosphere than there were ways to distribute the crystalizing compound in its solution. The crystalizing solution is not a closed system. When a subsystem is not closed, the second law does not apply to the subsystem, because entropy can be moved from the system to its environment.

Likewise, when life grows and evolves, there is no violation of the second law. The Earth is not a closed system. The Earth receives a steady stream of ordered energy from the Sun and emits highly disordered thermal radiation out into space. Thus, as in the case of crystal formation, there is no violation of the second law of thermodynamics in living or evolving things.

Evolution and Information

Many people reject the notion of evolution because they cannot believe that randomness can create non-randomness. And, phrased in that way, they are right. As a rule, pure randomness will not likely get you information or structure. However, evolution is so much more than randomness. Evolution is trial and error with memory. Randomness provides the trial. Selection tells evolution what works and what doesn't. Selection is what teaches evolution about reality.

Evolution and Mind

Alvin Plantinga, a renowned Christian theologian, argued that, if evolution is true, then thinking cannot be rational, and therefore, the conclusion that we evolved would be self-refuting.[14] According to his argument, evolution cares only about survival, not our beliefs per se. So long as our beliefs confer survival, evolutionary processes are happy. If evolution causes us to believe that we ought to pet tigers and that the best way to pet a tiger is to run away from it as fast as possible, then evolution has done its job. With these faulty beliefs, we would run from tigers and not get eaten.

Plantinga's argument rests on multiple misunderstandings of evolution and biology. First, beliefs do not magically float into our brains at random. The purpose of brains is to make inferences about our environment and about ourselves. Brains do this by creating abstractions from past experiences. Our concept of petting an animal comes from our experiences of approaching an animal and touching it with our hands. Likewise, our concept of escaping an animal are derived from experiences of moving nearer and further away from objects, animals, and peers.

---

[14] Plantinga, A. (1993). *Warrant and Proper Function.* Oxford University Press.

Objections

These concepts are not free-floating. They are conditioned by abstracting from experience.

Plantinga seems to assume that beliefs are not learned from experiences. He assumes that evolution somehow creates beliefs that result in the correct behavior, without any causal link between experience and belief. This, of course, is preposterous. Evolution created our belief formation mechanisms, and evolution very likely causes us to have cognitive biases that are not completely rational. But evolution does not create the beliefs themselves. Rather, we evolved brains that can make rational inferences from the patterns in our environment.

This is especially true of humans. People sometimes think that evolution wants to create more advanced animals such as humans rather than lesser animals such as crocodiles or sea sponges. But evolution has no mind. Evolution creates life that is well-suited to survive and reproduce in its respective niche. That is, crocodiles and sea sponges are no less evolved than humans. Each species evolves adaptations that make it better able to survive in its niche. Naked humans are not better able to survive in the Nile than crocodiles, not better able to survive the frigid waters of the Arctic than seals, nor better able to survive living in the ocean depths than sea sponges. What evolved strengths do humans possess?

The human advantage is the ability to learn to adapt to a new environment in less than a generation. With our big brains, we can learn to recognize the patterns in our environment. We can fashion tools and clothing, and we can learn to cultivate and hunt for food. This is why humans now live on every continent and are the most successful large animal on the planet. Thus, we did not evolve to have beliefs that work in a specific environment. We evolved to have brains that could acquire approximately accurate beliefs within a human lifetime.

The Argument from Reason

C.S. Lewis argued that mechanical systems might be built to function as if they could think, but they are intrinsically unable to do so. According to this argument, natural mechanisms lack the ability to think about things, that is, to recognize that a thought is about something in the world. For example, when we read a book about fungi, the connection between the printed words and fungi takes place in the human mind. From Lewis's perspective, the book itself is not about anything at all. All the "aboutness" in a book comes from a human mind. Likewise, he would argue, the structures in the human brain may encode information just like the words in a book or the bits in digital memory, but they have no intrinsic meaning. Lewis argues that, if naturalism is true, and if we are just mechanical beings, then our words and thoughts literally have no meaning, and the claim that "all the world is natural" would have no meaning.[15] Again, if Lewis's argument were correct, naturalism would be self-refuting because its conclusion would implicitly deny its own meaning.

This argument is interesting because it forces us to answer difficult questions about meaning. How can one piece of matter, like the human brain, have thoughts *about* another piece of matter?

---

[15] C.S. Lewis. *Miracles*. London & Glasgow: Collins/Fontana, 1947. Revised 1960.

The answer is that brains contain neural networks that are capable of learning and recognizing abstractions. We know that neural networks can do this because we can construct artificial neural networks that learn and recognize in the same way. For example, by looking at many trees—oaks, birches, sycamores, etc.—our young brains self-assemble a network of neurons that can visually recognize trees. When we speak of a tree, we are referring to "that which would be recognized by my tree-recognizing neural network." In this way, all our thoughts and utterances are linked to abstractions that we have formed by experience. This definition of semantic meaning is objective and consistent, so it resolves the problem that Lewis raised in his argument.

God Used Evolution

If the critic concedes that evolution works and explains the features we see in Earth's species, they could try to render evolution compatible with theism.

I think the most instinctive theistic response to the Counterargument from Design is simply to propose that we are dealing with a God who wanted to use evolution to create humanity. Since this God wants to use evolution, this new theory of divine design predicts the same evidence as unguided evolution. While nothing is impossible for God, this substitution is an instance of the kind of fine-tuning we discussed in Chapter 2. As we showed, one cannot fine-tune one's theory to match existing evidence without paying a corresponding penalty in the prior probability. If only one in a trillion designers would use evolution, then the prior probability of such a designer is a trillion times smaller.

To put it another way, absent a more refined argument, the objection fails because God using evolution to design us is precisely the equivalent of rolling a one on the trillion-sided die.

Consider the history of the debate between design and naturalistic evolution. When biologists relied exclusively on fossil evidence, advocates for design challenged the gaps in their fossil record. They believed that the Earth was much younger and that the fossils were not being dated correctly. That is, they implicitly denied the evolutionist's prediction of long timelines. In principle, the evolutionists could have turned out to be wrong. We could have found fossilized rabbits in Precambrian rock strata, and the theory of unguided evolution would have been falsified.

Design believers, even to this day, are largely convinced that God created most species by special creation, and that common descent is not true. In principle, we could have looked at the genomes of different species and found them to be inconsistent with common descent, thereby falsifying Darwinian evolution. In principle, we might have discovered species of birds that sing verses from the book of Psalms, disproving evolution. Yet, in every case, the evidence is consistent with unguided evolution, while design predicted anything but.

Before I move on, I want to tackle a particularly mind-bending framing of the God Used Evolution objection. Suppose the critic frames the objection as follows:

> *"I have fine-tuned my theory of God to assert that God created a natural world and aligned the initial conditions of the*

Objections

universe in such a way that natural evolution creates precisely the specific living things that we observe. I have effectively stolen all the predictions of natural evolutionary theory and incorporated them into my theory of design. Though I have fine-tuned my design theory, I now make correspondingly narrow predictions. In fact, I predict the existence of humans, whereas evolution does not!"

Initially, this framing might sound convincing, but upon closer examination, it falls apart. To start with, their theory does not predict humans. It has no predictive power of its own. If evolutionists and geneticists cannot predict humans specifically would evolve from their common ancestors, then neither can design advocates. The design advocate is merely further fine-tuning their theory to predict the humans we have already observed. If we were an alien species, like Klingons or Vulcans from *Star Trek*, the critic would have claimed to predict that species instead.

Also, to call evolution a prediction of their theory is disingenuous. To see why, it is important to describe the difference between a good theory and a bad one. I will use a simple mathematical example to illustrate this. Consider the graph in Figure 9 which depicts as-yet-unexplained data points.

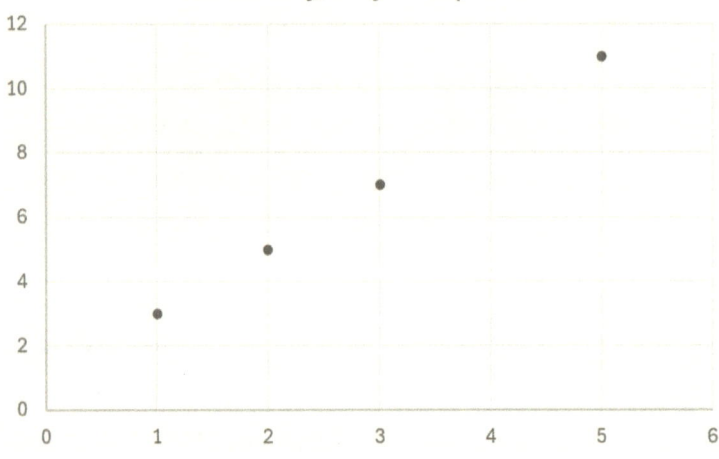

Figure 9—Data points, unexplained by theory

A good explanation for these data points will make predictions—extrapolations and interpolations as depicted in Figure 10. Of course, these predictions could turn out to be wrong, but if the next data point is consistent with our prediction, then we ought to become more confident in our theory.

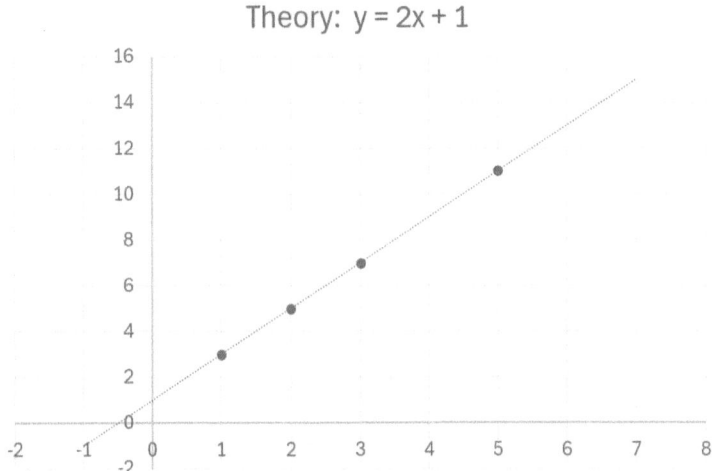

Figure 10—Data points explained by theory, with interpolations and extrapolations

This line theory has the axiom that $y = 2x + 1$. The line theory predicts that if we measure the value of y at $x = 4$, we should find $y = 9$. Finding y to be anything but 9 at $x = 4$ will falsify the line theory. And if we do find $y = 9$ at $x = 4$, then we should have greater confidence in line theory.

Though line theory is fine-tuned to match the first four data points, in exchange for that fine-tuning, it makes new predictions about what we will find next. As data points consistent with this theory appear, and data points inconsistent fail to appear, the line theory pays off its debt for fine-tuning.

What does a bad explanation look like?

Suppose an opponent of the $y = 2x + 1$ theory, we'll call him Wily, proposes an alternative "theory" that says, "The great Roadrunner has established data points will be at (1,3), (2,5), (3,7) and (5,11), and other values elsewhere." This illegitimate Roadrunner theory has done nothing but restate the data points we were trying to explain. That is, the axioms of Wily's Roadrunner theory are nothing but our observations so far. There is nothing about the Roadrunner that would *a priori* choose these points over any other we might have observed.

A theory that does not make predictions cannot be wrong, nor can it be right when future data points are measured. A theory that is compatible with any observation can never explain that observation. Nor should we become more confident in such a theory after the next data point is plotted, for the next data point was never predicted to be where it was found. Fake theories like Wily's can never pay their fine-tuning debts.

Now, suppose that, after thousands more observations, all our data points statistically line up with the line theory that $y = 2x + 1$. The success of this predictive theory will be such that we rationally trust the theory more than any individual data point. If an experimenter reports observing a data point at (500,1020) instead of (500,1001), we will tell them to go back to their lab and measure that point again, because we are still more confident in the line theory than in any single observation.

Eager to salvage the Roadrunner theory, Wily fine-tunes his theory to predict the line theory. "The great Roadrunner has established data points will accord with the line theory."

Again, this is not a prediction. There is nothing about the great Roadrunner that should prefer a linear theory to a quadratic one. And since the line theory is now even more trustworthy knowledge than any single observation data point, claiming to predict the line theory just restates what we already know. The new Roadrunner theory does not make any predictions or extrapolations.

I hope you can now see, by analogy, that a design theory that "predicts" evolutionary biology is just a Roadrunner theory. It is a fine-tuned theory that predicts only what we already know and nothing more.

Evolution Is Beautiful

Could it be that evolution was God's best choice?

If every possible designer, or most of them, would use evolution to create life, then the Counterargument from Design would fail. If the likelihood of finding the pattern of evolution were as likely (or nearly as likely) under theism, then the fact of evolution should not cause us to update our prior beliefs in the contest between naturalism and design.

As Darwin pointed out, an evolutionary solution has two things going for it: autonomy and aesthetics.

Autonomy is related to efficiency. For us humans, life is a constant battle against nature and entropy. In the era before automation, nothing was moved or sustained without continuous human effort. We were constantly sweeping, cleaning, repairing, preparing food, and fending off hostile animals or competitors. Mental activity is also costly to us. It takes effort and calories to plan, memorize, be vigilant, count our days, and count our provisions. Our families prosper only with care and with the creation of things that can serve future generations.

So, our labor-saving devices not only promote our survival and prosperity, but they also make us feel powerful. Imagine how powerful the maker of the first bow felt when he learned how to cast a projectile with greater force and deadly accuracy. When writing computer software, I often feel a sense of pride and power as I create a novel program to automate some cognitive drudgery.

Given evolution is autonomous and efficient, one might wonder whether it makes an attractive option to a designer. Alas, as discussed in the last chapter, infinitely powerful designers cannot claim efficiency as a benefit of choosing an evolutionary solution. Essentially, all actions are free for such a designer. If you ask a theist about how wasteful it seems to create an entire universe that is almost entirely uninhabitable, just to host some life forms on a tiny, blue planet, the theist is likely to point out that God is infinitely powerful, and creating an infinitely large universe is trivial for such a being.

We are surrounded by natural beauty. Canyons, rivers, volcanoes, cloud formations, stars, and planets. Living things are often described as miraculous. Earth's natural history is also beautiful in its own way. Charles Darwin concluded *On the Origin of Species* with reference to the aesthetics of evolution:

> *There is grandeur in this view of life, with its several powers, having been originally breathed by the Creator*

> *into a few forms or into one; and that, whilst this planet has gone circling on according to the fixed law of gravity, from so simple a beginning endless forms most beautiful and most wonderful have been, and are being evolved.*

Yet, Darwin's preceding sentence refers to the horror of the evolutionary process:

> *Thus, from the war of nature, from famine and death, the most exalted object which we are capable of conceiving, namely, the production of the higher animals, directly follows.*

Evolution requires death and suffering on an almost unimaginable scale. Most species that ever lived are now extinct, and almost every individual animal will die painfully from disease, starvation, or predation. If we are in no position to judge what true beauty is in the eye of the creator, then surely there are countless alternative worlds that have equal claim to divine beauty.

The Probability Does Not Exist

Not everyone accepts the Bayesian interpretation of probability. An alternative interpretation of probability—frequentism—defines probability as a statement of the number of positive events expected in large number of trials, as measured by past experience. Frequentists typically object to the notion of assigning a probability to a theory (or to a class of theories) as a whole.

Thus, a frequentist will likely reject the probabilistic conclusion of the Counterargument from Design on the basis that it is not what they would call a probability at all. Likewise, they would have to reject the Fine-Tuning Argument for the same reasons.

While the frequentist is rightly cautious about how prior probabilities are assigned in probabilistic arguments, I confess that I do not understand how to apply frequentism to the problem of rational belief. While there is nothing wrong with alternative definition or probability, relying on frequentism exclusively will put us into an epistemic straitjacket. Historical theories seem particularly problematic for a frequentist, because unique historical events occur only once. The probability that the legendary King Arthur drew a sword from a stone has no frequentist probability, because probabilities apply only to repeatable (and repeated) events.

In the Bayesian interpretation, rational belief corresponds to subjective probability. As a Bayesian, if I estimate, based on prior and evidence, that there is a 90% subjective probability that a theory will accurately predict experimental results, then I also *believe* with a 90% degree of confidence that the theory is true. But if I am a frequentist, and I cannot assign a probability to my theory *in toto*, then to what is my belief in the theory being calibrated, if anything?

If probability only has meaning in the narrow context of repeated, random trials, what should we rationally believe about King Arthur's sword in the stone? Or about the actions of General McArthur in World War II?

Presumably, frequentists have their own calculus for updating their confidence in their theories in response to evidence. No doubt some non-Bayesians will want to separate probability from rational belief, thereby insulating their beliefs from scientific evidence. However, I doubt that this strategy can be employed consistently. We believe the Earth is not flat, because the spheroid model of the Earth is more consistent with statistical observations of large distances on the Earth, distances between planets, Newtonian gravitation, the strength of the Earth's crust, and so on. If the probability of a theory as a whole cannot be nailed down by observations and frequentist statistics in this way, then how do we decide to rationally believe in a spheroidal Earth?

Natural Alternatives to Evolution

A critic might wonder whether the Counterargument from Design can be inverted, with naturalism and design trading places. If we can do this, the argument would be defeated, giving neither side an advantage. The reversed argument would assert that there are as many ways to create life in a natural universe as in a designed one. We already know of two ways life could form in a universe with simple, natural laws: evolution by natural selection and chance. Chance is so improbable that we can neglect it, but we should consider the possibility that natural universes could create life in a myriad of non-evolutionary ways.

Suppose there is some alternative to chance and evolution—I'll call it transmogrification. If this alternative were trillions of times more probable than evolution, then the Counterargument from Design would be defeated. However, transmogrification, if it existed, would have experimental consequences. Not only would our universe be teeming with life, but transmogrification would also be a process observable on Earth. Earth's species would transmogrify trillions of times faster than they could evolve. Yet, there is no sign of transmogrification in scientific research. Knowing this, we cannot invert the argument or call it a draw based on our ignorance of hypothetical transmogrification. If transmogrification exists, it cannot be trillions of times more probable than evolution.

Tuning Design to Observations

The modern synthesis of evolutionary biology has been tuned to match our observations. Darwin published *On the Origin of Species* before Gregor Mendel presented his theory of inheritance. Even after its publication, Mendel's work languished in obscurity for another four decades, and the theory of genetics would not be integrated with Darwinian evolution until the 20th century. Since then, biologists have catalogued millions of species, better understood speciation, and learned much about mutation rates. In light of our knowledge of how life formed on Earth, contemporary evolutionary theory has been continuously refined and updated. We might try to defeat the Counterargument from Design by supposing that we should do the same for design. Yes, a designer might have designed the world in a fashion that does not resemble what we observe, but can the same not be said for evolutionary naturalism?

If this objection can be sustained, then we should not be comparing a generic theory of design to a refined theory of evolution. Perhaps we should compare a refined theory of design to a refined theory of evolution, in which case the odds might be more favorable for design theories.

The first thing to note is that, inasmuch as we can fine-tune our models to the scientific data, this has already been done for design. Design is completely parasitic on the natural sciences for its explanation of the details of what we observe in evolution.

The Counterargument from Design is not asking why life evolved the way it did on Earth. The argument is asking why life evolved at all when it could have arisen via an infinite number of alternatives that could not evolve. As explained in the previous section, evolution seems to be the only likely way to get life under naturalism, but it is obviously not the only way to create life under design. To overcome the Counterargument from Design, advocates for design must explain why designers must prefer evolving life to designing it by other means, why the countless valuable worlds that can only be arrived at via design are devalued.

Inscrutability

Inscrutability is the notion that citing a probability does not accurately capture our relationship to some aspect of knowledge. We might think of it as alluding to unknown unknowns instead of known unknowns.

When we say the odds of heads or tails on a fair coin are 50-50, we seem to be saying something more precise than when we say the probability that humans will colonize Mars or employ nuclear fusion for electric power by the year 2100. In the first case, we understand the physics of coin flips and the nature of our unknowns, whereas in the projections about future scientific and technical advance, we do not understand the unknowns. To put this another way, we know what the probability distribution is for fair coin flips, but we do not know the probability distributions for future technical advances. We can say we know the probability of getting tails on the next flip of a fair coin is 50% because we understand its mechanism. Yet, the probability of employing fusion power by 2100 is somewhere between 10% and 90% because we do not fully understand the technical and economic hurdles. While both projections might equate to 50-50 odds, the two statements seem to be different in kind. The prospect of fusion power this century is more inscrutable.

To apply inscrutability to God would be to argue that we know so little about the designer that the probability that God would create a world that appears evolved is anywhere between 0% and 100%.

Personally, I do not find the inscrutability argument convincing, and the best analogy I can give will bring us back to a trillion-sided-die analogy. Suppose I cast my trillion-sided die. The randomness of the die roll is illusory. In truth, I have imparted momentum and spin to the die, and the gravity, air currents, and imperfections in the tabletop will precisely determine the outcome of the roll. The perceived randomness is just a way for us to express our ignorance of these microphysical details. For all we know, given the microphysical details, there might be a 100% chance that we will roll a one on the trillion-sided die.

What licenses us in taking the roll of a one as a one-in-a-trillion improbability is that we see no reason why the other outcomes are impossible, and we have no more reason to favor one conceivable outcome of the roll than any other. Likewise, it is true that, for all we know, an all-powerful God must design life that appears evolved. But it is also true that, for all we know, an all-powerful God must design life to resemble My Little Pony or any of an infinity of worlds that do not look evolved. And since there are vastly many more ways that a God can create non-evolved life, and we have no *a priori* reason to favor one over the other, we cannot consistently grant a high probability to the theory that the designer wanted an evolved world.

Infinities

The dice game example that I used to illustrate Bayesian inference in Chapter 2 is simple and innocuous. But one may well ask how the calculation might be possible if both dice have an infinite number of sides. The mathematics of infinity generally precludes us making sense of ratios. For example, consider the set of whole numbers, 1, 2, 3, and so on. There are infinitely many whole numbers. Now consider the set of whole numbers that are evenly divisible by 3, e.g., 3, 6, 9, 12....

Naively, we expect that there are three times as many whole numbers as there are multiples of three. Indeed, in any finite, contiguous subset of whole numbers, this is the case. There are about three times as many whole numbers in the range 1–1,000,000 as there are multiples of three in that range.

But when we consider the entire set of whole numbers and the entire set of multiples of three, we find there are infinitely many of both, and we cannot say there are three times as many whole numbers as multiples of three. The infinites are of the same order, and a simple ratio will not distinguish the two.

Of course, probability theory is quite capable of working with continuous values within a finite range. If I knew only that a submarine is located somewhere in the Atlantic, I could sensibly assign probabilities of 50% to it laying in the Eastern Atlantic and 50% to it laying in the West. But if the Atlantic were infinitely large, and if the submarine could be anywhere, it would become difficult if not impossible to apply the logic of probability to the location of the submarine.

Thus, a skeptic can reasonably question whether such limitations in the logic of probability apply to the infinite number of possible worlds contemplated in the Counterargument from Design. As it turns out, this limitation does not apply to the counterargument. In our current theory of physics, there is a finite number of ways to arrange a finite amount of matter and energy in a finite volume. This limit is called the Bekenstein Bound.[16] For any finite planet that is subject to physical law, there is a maximum number of ways of arranging the matter and energy of the planet. Physics and evolution predict that only a very small proportion of these configurations are remotely probable. This means that there is a finite number of worlds that can evolve on a mindless physical substrate.

---

[16] Bekenstein, Jacob D. (1981). *Universal upper bound on the entropy-to-energy ratio for bounded systems.* Physical Review D. 23 (2): 287–298.

However, the same limitation does not apply to divinely designed worlds. An infinite creator can violate the physical laws we see. For example, God could create creatures with souls that have infinitely many psychic variations or employ biology that is not subject to the Bekenstein Bound. This flexibility to create infinitely many worlds in the case of design only strengthens the Counterargument from Design. While the ratio of two infinite numbers may be indeterminate, dividing a finite number by an infinite one will result in zero.

Thus, appealing to the infinities involved in these possible worlds will only amplify the argument.

The Measure Problem

Probability analysis always involves some assumptions. The Counterargument from Design relies upon the assumption that God has many more options when designing a world than when evolving a world. The more options God has with design, the more powerful the argument becomes. But precisely how should we estimate or measure the number of possible worlds that can be designed?

One approach to measuring distinct possibilities is to count physically distinct worlds. For example, suppose that God evolves every species on Earth, but elects to design cats independent from all other species, such that cats have their own, wholly unrelated genome. That is, God singles out the cat from among Earth's two million species for custom development. To design this custom cat, God also picks out just one of the trillions of unique genomes and biochemistries that would result in something resembling a cat. At the atomic level, this choice of genome multiplies the number of possible designed worlds by trillions. This is because not only can God choose any number of Earth's two million species for custom development, but he also has trillions of chemical ways of putting together each of those chosen custom designs.

Yet, human beings generally do not care about the microscopic differences that result from the choices they make. For example, there are millions more ways of arranging 250 grains of rice on a plate than there are ways of arranging a single tuna steak on a plate, but you would not thereby conclude that a random stranger was millions of times more likely to eat a rice dish than a tuna steak. We choose meals to create variety, for the taste, for the texture, and for their nutritional value. The statistical permutations of microscopic arrangements of food are irrelevant to our choice of meals.

In Chapter 4, a few of the large numbers of designed alternatives might simply be irrelevant to the designer's palette of choices. For example, if God wants to create cats, the molecular composition of cats may well be an irrelevant criterion, and the fact that cats can be composed in a vast number of ways at the molecular level doesn't necessarily make them more likely objects of creation than simpler creatures.

If we take this objection to its extreme, we can imagine a scenario in which God's only criterion of choice is making the world appear evolved or making the world appear designed, with 50-50 odds. In this extreme case, the Counterargument from Design all but dissolves.

Objections

However, there are good reasons to think that this most extreme objection is not a good one. First, humans do not care how our rice is arranged on our dinner plates, because, not only can we not easily measure it, but we also have no way of extrapolating the consequences. If, like God, we could foresee the long-term effects of the microscopic arrangements of matter that we create, then microscopic factors would become interesting criteria for us.

Second, even ignoring any microscopic factors, it seems preposterous that the only thing God would care about is whether or not a world had wholly evolved. Even humans have a broader palette of criteria than this. Humans care about humor, justice, mathematics, product design, gossip, relationships, sport, poetry, cinematography, crafting, and architecture, to name just a handful of things. We have created a vast array of visual artistic genres, from Dadaism to classical sculpture. Humans have thousands of rituals and symbols, and hundreds of languages. All these wonderful things are inventions created by our relatively feeble human brains. Are we really to believe that the aesthetic tastes of every infinitely powerful creator is dwarfed by that of humans?

In evolved worlds, there is only one value or utility, one formula. Life is in constant, mortal struggle to outbreed its competition. But a divine designer can create a world wherein humans and other animals can be vastly smarter and more artistic, where all life can participate in creating value through knowledge, dialogue, and artistic practice. In divinely designed worlds, all life can cooperate to maximize value without the need for destructive competition.

When humans imagined what the designer's purpose must be, they had to fit their mythology to what they observed in nature. We observed struggle in the world, so we imagined that the gods struggled amongst themselves or wanted humanity to struggle against nature. In the Abrahamic religions, humans struggle because they are cast out from the paradise of an obviously designed and cooperative world. But if we were imagining all the worlds that a deity might create, there are seemingly an infinite number of things for which a designer might optimize the world, and only an infinitesimal sliver of such possibilities would appear evolved.

Naturalism Is Poorly Defined

I defined natural metaphysics as the theory that the fundamental laws of reality are simple and non-mental. This definition is a generalization of the scientific picture of the world. The alternative to naturalism is supernaturalism. A supernatural world contains some features wherein mental properties are fundamental. For example, in most metaphysical interpretations, ghosts lack material bodies and are not the result of chemical reactions or simple physics. Their souls or mentalities are fundamental and not made of subcomponents. As mentioned earlier, there is nothing wrong with supernatural explanations in principle, so long as the supernatural theories make predictions that can be tested. The magic of Harry Potter's universe is supernatural, but it is also perfectly reliable, testable, and predictive.

As a starting point, these definitions can serve us adequately. However, if we were weighing every possible natural metaphysics against every possible supernatural metaphysics, we would likely require definitions that are far more precise.

Let's slice up the categories of natural and supernatural metaphysics into distinct categories. The first distinction I want to make concerns realities that contain both natural laws and supernatural features. This is the type of reality that many people believe we are living in. They believe the world is mostly natural and physical, but there are additional entities, interventions, and causes that are supernatural.

My next distinction concerns apparently natural realities, that is, realities in which science sees no sign of the supernatural. Again, many people today believe that we live in a supernatural reality, but that science cannot see the supernatural parts.

Finally, some, but not all, supernatural realities will contain a divine creator.

With these distinctions, we can draw a Venn diagram of the possible metaphysical realities, as shown in Figure 11. The diagram contains some metaphysical notions that we might at first have failed to consider. For example, there may be some natural worlds in which seemingly supernatural things occur. As science fiction author Arthur C. Clark once wrote, "Any sufficiently advanced technology is indistinguishable from magic." The diagram also includes realities that are natural, that appear natural (because the divine interventions are so subtle) yet are nonetheless divinely designed.

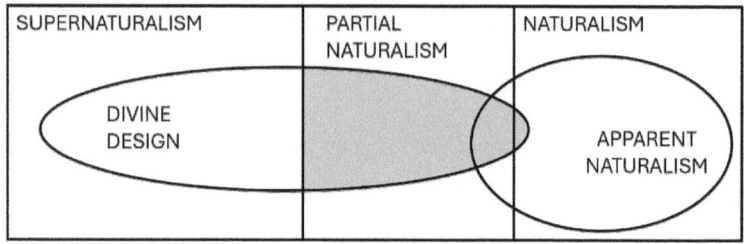

Figure 11—A Venn diagram depicting categories of metaphysical theory

The Counterargument from Design is, roughly speaking, comparing the number of possible natural life-bearing worlds to some corresponding number of supernatural worlds. Finding that the number of natural worlds is far smaller, and finding our world seemingly naturally created, should lead us to believe that naturalism is more likely. However, if we are hoping to apply the argument across every kind of natural metaphysics, we will need to imagine and then quantify all the conceivable natural metaphysical possibilities, and that is a tall order.

Fortunately, the Counterargument from Design need not look at every variant of natural and supernatural metaphysics. Instead, we can consider all those worlds that contain the natural laws of our own universe, whether entirely natural or partially supernatural, whether apparently natural or not. After making this restriction, the naturalistic side of the ledger includes all the biospheres that can evolve, unguided, in our physical universe. As far as we know, all the natural worlds with our physics will have the traits of evolutionary biology.[17] The supernatural

---

[17] The only exceptions will be worlds designed by finite, naturally evolved designers, and these worlds will look quite different from worlds created by a divine designer.

side of the ledger includes all those biospheres that feature our physical laws plus supernatural divine design of any kind. With this constraint, we can more confidently employ the Counterargument from Design laid out in the previous chapters.

Summary

In this chapter, I have anticipated a dozen criticisms of the Counterargument from Design. No doubt more objections will be raised by others, and this is a good thing. If there are flaws in the argument, we should want to know what they are.

If the Counterargument from Design garners interest, I expect sharper minds than my own will produce better critiques and counter-critiques than my own. The Fine-Tuning Argument, a similar evidential argument, has already inspired hundreds of academic papers, for and against.

Ultimately, the Counterargument from Design is motivated by the asymmetry between naturalism and supernatural design. If naturalism is true, we must find certain features in the world. We must find that life can evolve unguided and that living things must have biochemical computers and biochemical communications networks in their bodies. Under supernaturalism, none of these things need be true. We might have discovered that evolution did not happen or that evolution was impossible. We might have discovered that brains have no computing ability and that souls were the only explanation. Things could have been different, but they were not. It is difficult to devise an objection that makes this asymmetry go away.

7
Cosmic Fine-Tuning

"Imagination will often carry us to worlds that never were. But without it we go nowhere."

— *Carl Sagan*

In the 20th century, as our understanding of physics and the cosmos matured, scientists noticed that the strengths of the fundamental forces of nature seemed exquisitely balanced. Without this delicate balance, there would be no stars and no life as we know it. If we assume that the strengths of these forces are random variables, then it seems a fortunate coincidence that these forces have the strengths that they do. Indeed, Fine-Tuning Arguments typically claim that the probability of these random constants aligning in so blessed a fashion is less than 1 in 10^{100}. This fortunate coincidence is the basis of a theological argument called the Fine-Tuning

Argument. According to the argument, the best explanation for this lucky set of physical constants is divine intervention.[18]

The Fine-Tuning Argument is superficially like the Counterargument from Design. Both arguments use probability theory, and both involve extreme coincidences. Moreover, anyone dismayed by the Counterargument from Design is likely to cite the Fine-Tuning Argument as a counterweight. As we shall see, there are important differences between the two arguments that render the Fine-Tuning Argument much weaker by comparison.

A Brief History of the Universe

In a universe governed by natural laws, life can only exist if the laws of physics and the initial conditions permit complex chemistry. To store and employ a genetic code, nature must have a sufficient density of stable building blocks, as the right amount of energy to keep the machinery running over millions of years. The best physical model of our universe has all these ingredients. The model combines the Standard Model of particle physics, Albert Einstein's general theory of relativity, and our current theory of Big Bang cosmology. The whole thing can be written on one letter-sized piece of paper.

The formulas in the model describe the four fundamental forces—electromagnetism, the weak nuclear force, the strong nuclear force, and gravity—as well as the masses and interactions between the fundamental

---

[18] I capitalize "Fine-Tuning Argument" when I refer to the theological argument for a cosmic designer, to distinguish it from more general references to fine-tuning in physics or probabilistic reasoning.

particles. The equations describe the complex structure of reality, and they incorporate about twenty-six physical constants that describe the relative strengths of the forces and the relative mass of the particles. These physical constants have been calibrated in numerous laboratory experiments.

Our universe was once very hot, very dense, and expanding rapidly. As the universe expanded and cooled, it created clouds of hydrogen that condensed into stars and galaxies. Nuclear fusion in the cores of these stars created heavier elements, like carbon and oxygen. And when the heaviest stars exploded at the end of their lives, they created yet heavier chemical elements and scattered them across space. Earth and the life that dwells upon it were created out of this star stuff. These heavier elements provide the chemistry necessary for geology, water, and life itself. Our Sun is a typical, long-lived star. The Sun has burned for billions of years, providing the Earth with a steady source of free energy, powering chemical processes across our planet. Without all this chemistry and energy, life as we know it could not exist.

Curiously, if the parameters that describe our physical model are changed even a little, the story of our universe unfolds very differently. If the expansion of the universe is too fast, then hydrogen clouds do not collapse into stars and there is no chemistry. If gravity is too strong, the universe collapses before stars can form. If the nuclear forces and masses are not balanced as they are, then stars will not produce sufficient carbon for organic life. If the electromagnetic force were too strong, heavy elements cannot form and there is no chemistry.

The question is, what explains the balance of the forces of nature that has led to the formation of complex chemistry and life on Earth?

If the parameters in our models of particle physics and the Big Bang are assumed to be independent, random numbers, then we seem to be here only because of a bizarre coincidence. This problem is known as the fine-tuning problem.

Physicists and philosophers use the term fine-tuning in different ways. For physicists, it is a technical term for unexplained relationships in the laws of physics. However, philosophers, most notably Christian theologians, see the fine-tuning problem as an opportunity to construct an argument for theism or for some non-natural explanation for why we are here. These sorts of fine-tuning arguments are similar in structure to the Counterargument from Design. They argue that, if the parameters describing the laws of physics are random, then we find ourselves in a statistically improbable situation. Yet, if the universe is designed for life or even for humanity itself, then the cosmic coincidence is easily explained.

Many theists regard this cosmic Fine-Tuning Argument as one of the strongest arguments for the existence of a designer. If the Counterargument from Design should cause us to think that design is improbable, might the Fine-Tuning Argument work as a counterbalance? What are the similarities and differences between the fine-tuning argument and the Counterargument from Design?

Objections to Cosmic Fine-Tuning Arguments

There are many objections to the Fine-Tuning Argument. The first objection comes from physics. Physical constants are not independent parameters, and some analysis suggests that large parts of the parameter space are friendly to life. The second and more powerful objection is statistical. Because we cannot observe ourselves not to exist, there is an observer selection bias that nullifies the inference. Indeed, after compensating for this bias, what remains is a weak argument for naturalism.

Physics

There are four known forces in nature: electromagnetic, weak nuclear, strong nuclear, and gravity. These forces have characteristic ranges and strengths. Gravity and electromagnetism are forces with infinite range, whereas nuclear forces have very small ranges on the scale of atomic nuclei. Electromagnetic force is responsible for chemistry and electromagnetic radiation (e.g., light, radio waves, x-rays,). The weak nuclear force is responsible for radioactive decay. The weak nuclear force and electromagnetism couldn't be more different at the energies humans encounter every day. Yet, in the 1970s, physicists devised a theory that unified the weak nuclear force and electromagnetism. The two forces, though seemingly very different, were aspects of the same single force: the electro-weak force. At high energies and temperatures, such as those at the birth of our universe, the two forces would have been indistinguishable. As the universe cooled, the symmetry between the two forces was broken, resulting in two seemingly very different laws of physics.

The discovery of electro-weak unification has been one of the great successes of physics in the 20th century. Today, physicists are striving to unify the remaining forces. Theories of grand unification would unite the electro-weak force and the strong nuclear force, while so-called "theories of everything" would complete the unification of all the forces in the universe.

From this history lesson, we can infer that the strengths of the forces of nature and the masses of the fundamental particles in the universe are unlikely to be random variables. Instead, there are as yet undetermined patterns that connect the parameters describing the cosmos. This means that, to the extent that a Fine-Tuning Argument assumes the constants are independent random variables, it proceeds from an improbable premise.

The Fine-Tuning Argument also depends on the assumption that universes unlike our own will be inhospitable to life. A kernel of this argument is surely reasonable. We can likely construct variations of our laws of physics that would not support life as we know it. However, there are critical weaknesses in this argument. The first weakness is that writing down a theory and understanding its consequences are two different things. Making detailed predictions from a model is challenging and time-consuming. Decades after the Standard Model was invented, there are still consequences of the theory for our own universe that we are struggling to calculate. String theories, despite their beauty and promise as theories of everything, have languished because we do not have the ability to compute their consequences. Still, physicists have created crude simulations of alternative universes, finding that a relatively large fraction of these hypothetical universes are hospitable to life. Perhaps the universe is not as fine-tuned as it may appear.[19]

---

[19] Stenger, Victor J. *The Fallacy of Fine-Tuning*. Chapter 13. Prometheus Books, 2011.

Thus, the claim that if the laws of physics were different, the universe could not support life is not on solid ground. The claim relies at least partly on our ignorance of the consequences of alternative laws of physics.

Multiverses

There are also physical theories that may explain why the universe is as we observe it to be. Physicists have long known that the universe is extremely homogeneous on the largest observable scales. In every direction, the universe seems to have about the same temperature. The leading explanation for this homogeneity is a theory called cosmic inflation. According to this theory, the universe underwent rapid expansion in the first instant after the Big Bang. Our measurements of the cosmic microwave background radiation are consistent with inflation. Interestingly, the simplest theories of cosmic inflation are multiverse models. In these models, the instability that caused our universe to inflate is akin to the instabilities in a glass of beer. Just as many bubbles form in a glass of beer, many universes form from the primordial vacuum. And in each cosmic bubble, the laws of physics may differ. If this theory is correct, then the cosmos makes every kind of universe. Even if most of these universes could not support life, as long as one or a few do support life, the fine-tuning problem is solved. After all, we can only find ourselves in a universe compatible with life, so it is no surprise that we should find ourselves in a universe like this one.

Another physical theory that might explain why the universe has the parameters that it does is Lee Smolin's evolutionary universe hypothesis. According to this theory, black holes create new universes. If the universes created by black holes are similar to the universes that gave birth to the black holes, then statistically, the universes that give birth to the greatest number of black holes would also birth the greatest number of new universes. In this way, universes with laws of physics most friendly to black holes would outcompete universes with alternative laws of physics. Conditions in our universe are particularly favorable for the creation of black holes—conditions favorable for star formation are also conditions more favorable for life.

Though these theories are still speculative, they illustrate that physicists have alternative explanations for cosmic fine-tuning. Moreover, these explanations were developed to explain physics problems, not merely evade philosophical arguments.

Probability Theory

At first, the Fine-Tuning Argument resembles the Counterargument from Design. We can write down a Bayesian argument for fine-tuning that appears to function in the same way. However, the Fine-Tuning Argument suffers from an observer selection effect that violates important assumptions of probabilistic inference.[20]

The great physicist Sir Arthur Eddington devised a famous illustration of the observer selection effect. Suppose you cast a fishing net into a lake, and upon withdrawing the net you find that the smallest fish in your catch are 10 inches long. You are about to conclude that the smallest fish in the lake are 10 inches long when you notice your error. The holes in your net are just small enough that 10-inch fish cannot escape, but smaller fish can pass

---

[20] For an in-depth explanation of these issues, see Sober, E. *The Design Argument.* Cambridge University Press, 2018.

through. Thus, your net is blind to fish smaller than 10 inches, and you cannot infer from your catch the size of the smallest fish in the lake. Your observation of fish sizes has selected only fish that are 10 inches or larger.

The Fine-Tuning Argument suffers from precisely this kind of bias because we cannot possibly observe ourselves to exist in a universe incompatible with our existence.

We can visually represent the Counterargument from Design in a similar way. If we give equal priors to naturalism and design, then we grant each a 50% share of the whole. We then subdivide the design segment into a very small segment representing the small prior probability that the designer creates evolved life, and a much larger segment representing the large prior that the designer would create something obviously designed.

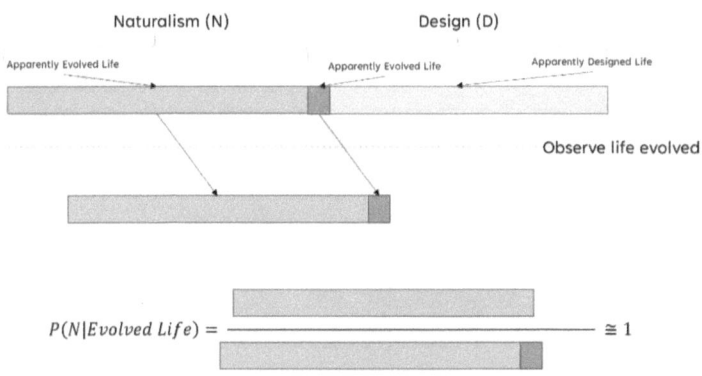

Much like in the dice game in Chapter 2, we conclude that it is much more probable (indeed, almost certain) that life arose naturally, without design.

Naively, we might think that precisely the same recipe can be used for the Fine-Tuning Argument. Again, granting equal 50% priors to naturalism and design theism, we subdivide the prior for naturalism into a piece representing the probability that our variant of naturalism is compatible with life, and a piece representing variations of naturalism that are lifeless. If we accept the controversial premise of cosmic Fine-Tuning Arguments, and grant that the prior probability of fine-tuned, life-friendly, natural universes is small, then the life-friendly segment of the prior for naturalism is very small.

On the design side of the prior, we might suppose that the subdivision is coarser. Perhaps there is a two-thirds prior probability that God will create a life-bearing universe. The result is a visual representation like this one:

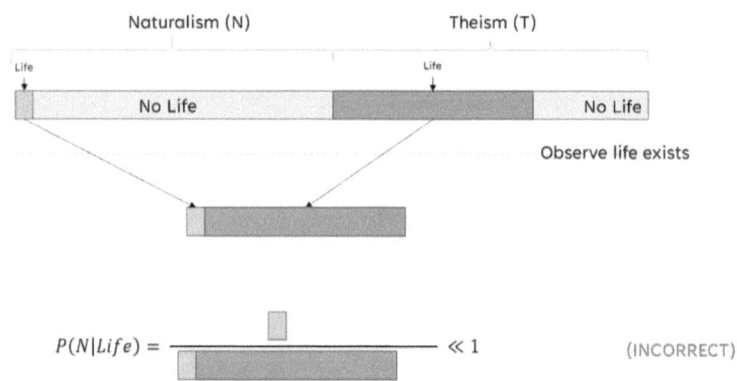

After observing that life exists, we compute the ratio of the prior probability segments and conclude that the probability that naturalism is true is very small. However, this conclusion is flawed. The mistake is due to the observer selection effect.

Within our visual representation of Bayesian inferences, we assume that the bar at the top is a true prior probability for the kinds of outcomes we might observe. However, because we cannot observe ourselves not to exist, the parts of the bar representing lifeless universes cannot be part of the prior. Instead, we have to rescale our bars on the assumption that life does exist. This results in the ratio of probabilities at the start of the inference looking exactly the same at the end. The posterior probabilities for naturalism and design are the same as the prior probabilities, and we learn nothing. Just like the fisherman who sees no fish smaller than the holes in his net learns nothing about the small fish in the lake, we learn nothing about the probability of life-friendly universes by this observation.

Thus, even if we accept the dubious claim that the universe is fine-tuned, the Fine-Tuning Argument is fallacious. In fact, once we look more closely, the Fine-Tuning Argument ends up supporting naturalism, albeit only weakly.

While all life in a naturalistic universe is constrained by physical compatibility with its environment, the same is not true of a designed universe. In a designed universe, life can be supernatural and defy the constraints of physics. Angels and ghosts are a form of life that can exist independent of physical laws. The fact that all known life is physical ends up supporting naturalism.

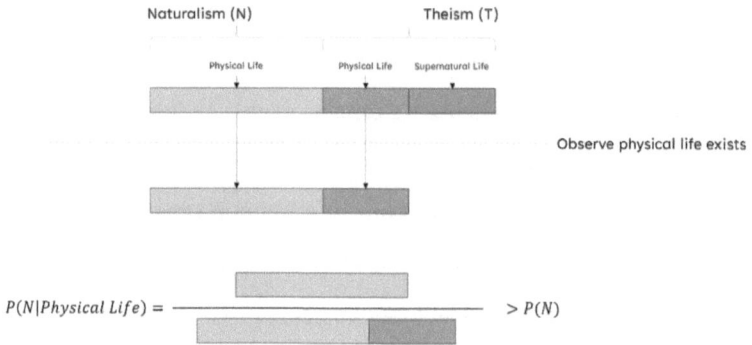

We can confirm that the counterargument from design does not suffer from the same fallacy. Every part of the prior probability is observable, in principle. We could easily have observed ourselves to be designed beings, so there is no observer selection effect.

A Multiversal Escape Route?

As we have seen, the Fine-Tuning Argument is fallacious, so we need not devise an escape route for naturalism. However, the fact that Fine-Tuning Arguments are fallacious is little known. Consequently, many commentators prefer to invoke multiverse theories to escape the Fine-Tuning Argument. Their reasoning is, if the multiverse creates every kind of universe, then of course, life-friendly universes can be found somewhere in the multiverse.

Though the cosmic fine-tuning argument cannot counterbalance the Counterargument from Design, defenders of design theories might wonder whether something analogous to a multiverse argument can save them from the Counterargument from Design. If God creates every kind of universe, including evolved universes, does that defuse the argument?

As you may surmise, realizing a multitude of designed life cannot resolve the problem for design theorists. Realizing every possible design merely transforms the epistemic prior probability distribution into a population distribution. That is, the prior probability that God would create life through evolution is transformed into the prior probability that we find ourselves on an evolved world in the multitude of designs.

Summary

Though the cosmic Fine-Tuning Argument superficially resembles the Counterargument from Design, it is fallacious.

8
Conclusion

> *"For small creatures such as we,*
> *the vastness is bearable only through love."*
>
> — *Carl Sagan*

The Counterargument from Design is a new way of looking at an old argument. Theists and atheists have long recognized that evolutionary biology paints a picture that seems generally at odds with important parts of theology. To this day, popular apologists for religion appear in the media to cast doubt on the science of evolutionary biology, arguing that divine intent and divine manipulation must appear somewhere in the human story. Atheists, for their part, generally believe that evolution removes the need for life's creator, and thereby makes God seem that much more absurd.

The Counterargument from Design places this old argument into a statistically interesting form. If the counterargument can be sustained, it is devastating to the kinds of theism that believers desire, namely, the kinds of theism in which humans derive significance from their creator.

I do not expect a unanimous judgment on the merits of the Counterargument from Design. If we are being Bayesian about the history of argumentation, we should infer from the history of past theological (and atheistic) arguments that good arguments move the needle of faith just a little, while bad arguments persist as rationalizations for what people want to believe. However the argument is ultimately judged, I hope that it gives clear thinkers some more points of leverage in understanding how the science of evolutionary biology ought to affect our beliefs about design.

Political Implications

If the Counterargument from Design does end up influencing public discourse, it will directly affect several political questions. The first of these concerns science education. In the United States, the teaching of evolution in schools has long been a point of political contention. The Bible states that the world was created in six days directly by God, only a few thousand years ago. Biology and geology plainly contradict this literal reading of the Bible. If one's belief system demands adherence to a literal interpretation of an ancient text, then scientific evidence to the contrary is simply irrelevant.

Fortunately, most theists are not biblical literalists, and they are unwilling to reject ironclad scientific evidence to save a purely literal interpretation of Genesis. Religious people usually find a way to harmonize their interpretation of religious text with scientific evidence. Indeed, religious people often declare that understanding science only enhances their appreciation for divine creation. As I mentioned in my introduction, the Catholic Church now endorses the teaching of evolutionary biology, and Catholic universities teach accredited courses in evolutionary biology. Meanwhile, the Clergy Letter Project has amassed more than 16,000 signatures from Christian and Jewish clergy asserting compatibility between their respective religious doctrines and evolutionary biology.

But what if biblical literalists are correct that there is no compatibility between scripture and science? This, after all, is what the Counterargument from Design argues. Will believers still side with scientific evidence if it costs them their faith? To the extent that the Counterargument from Design triggers this kind of dilemma, it will likely make it more difficult for science educators to bring evolution into the classroom.

The Counterargument is also politically relevant to the debate about reproductive choice. Those with a naturalistic view of the world see no harm in terminating a pregnancy before a fetus has the cognitive capacity to suffer, especially if the health and choice of the mother are countervailing considerations.

While there are some nonreligious arguments against reproductive choice, they are relatively weak. For example, some people are simply uncomfortable with the lack of simple criteria for the moral acceptability of abortion. Those who cannot tolerate ambiguity might simply decide that a fertilized egg is just as much a human being as a living adult, and therefore, abortion is morally unacceptable in all circumstances. There also seems to be a contingent of people whose goal in restricting abortion is to reduce the number of single-parent families (and the sociological problems that they attribute to a lack of traditional family structure). If only we all took sex and parenthood much more seriously, they say, if only we return to traditional family values, then we might reduce the number of out-of-wedlock pregnancies and absent fathers. At the same time, advocates for this view also want to restrict access to birth control, because birth control gives license to sex outside of traditional marriage. I have seen no evidence that anti-choice policy of this type has any chance of success.

Still, most frequently, the rejection of reproductive choice is tied to a religious worldview. If human beings and human reproduction were intended as part of God's design, then it is morally questionable to interfere with this natural process in any way. So long as evolution remains compatible with a religious worldview, the divine intention argument may still be persuasive. The Counterargument from Design has obvious relevance here. Unlike arguments that target theism more broadly, the counterargument addresses divine intent. Evolution tells us that human life was not intended, and this strips away any argument that is based on divine intent.

The Meaning of Life

Religions that espouse faith in a God who intended humanity are well-equipped to create a sense of meaning in the lives of their adherents. Their message is a powerful one. We are not merely animals. We are special, magical creatures. We belong here, and by embracing the divine purpose, we allow divinity to guide us to become better people. Ultimately, our soul will survive the death of our physical bodies.

The promise of life after death is a major selling point. However, an aspirational identity that integrates your daily thoughts and activities with a sense of divine purpose is also very powerful. For people who live this way, every choice, every good deed is imbued with a holy spirit. Thinking in this way may add a layer of beauty to otherwise mundane aspects of life. One need not be a biblical literalist or evolution denier to feel such effects.

The Counterargument from Design does not disprove the existence of all gods, but it does strip away divine intent, so I suspect the counterargument threatens the meaning of life for most people in traditional theistic religions.

Yet, it would be a mistake to assume that a sense of meaning and significance cannot be found in a naturalistic worldview. To be sure, modern secular living is often devoid of religious meaning. Most secularists are ardent consequentialists and utilitarians. Morally, they are deeply concerned with fairness and the avoidance of material harm and suffering. At the same time, there has long been a sense that contemporary secular culture is facing a meaning crisis. People do not feel special nor part of any grand narrative. The world feels like a giant machine, and we only do good by perfectly executing a moral cost-benefit analysis. We are wracked with pessimism about the human project, with its pollution and injustice.

For my part, I believe that meaning and significance can be found in a natural world. We simply need an aspirational identity that is compatible with a scientific way of looking at the world. We need a humanism that appreciates the virtue of clear thinking and rationality, not just the consequentialist benefits of science. We should recognize that humans are beautiful and glorious, at their best, and that we should be kind to them and honor them. Part of the crown jewels of our civilization is our hard-won understanding of our universe and our own natural history.

Index

A

abiogenesis · 59
abortion · 152
angels · 66, 67, 87, 145
ATP · 63

B

Bayes' Theorem · 17, 30, 41, 49, 50
Bayesian epistemology · 30, 31, 100
Bayesian inference · 14, 17, 26, 37, 125, 144
Behe, Michael · 74, 75
Bekenstein Bound · 126, 127
Big Bang · 138, 141

C

chance · 43, 44, 48, 49, 51
common descent · 62, 83
cosmic fine-tuning · 9, 135, 138, 142, 144, 146, 147
Cosmological Argument · 9, 105

D

Darwin, Charles · 2, 4, 8, 11, 41, 44, 59, 77, 97, 117, 118, 119, 122
designers, finite · 78

E

Eddington, Arthur · 142
efficiency · 117, 118
evolution, ingredients · 57
evolution, predictions · 60
　common composition · 63
　common descent · 62
　descent · 62
　knowledge is learned · 65
　long timelines · 64
　number of species · 64
　survival as utility · 64
　vulnerability to physics · 66
evolution, teaching · 73, 150
explanations, promissory · 89

F

Fine-Tuning Argument · 14, 100, 103, 120, 136, 138, 142, 143, 145, 146, 147
fine-tuning, probability · 37, 38, 39, 41, 42
fossil record · 42, 59, 61, 76, 77
frequentism · 119, 120, 121

G

Genesis · 3, 56, 64, 66, 85, 87, 89, 98, 151
God of the Gaps · 76
Gould, Stephen J. · 101

H

Haldane, J.B.S. · 77

I

idealism · 102, 103
inscrutability · 123
intelligent design · 7, 51, 54, 56, 73, 75, 77, 78, 81, 83
intelligent design, movement · 73
irreducible complexity · 74

J

jigsaw puzzle analogy · 32

L

Lewis, C.S. · 110

M

maze puzzle analogy · 45, 46, 47,
  48, 49, 50, 51, 52, 53, 54,
  55, 56, 57, 62, 64, 68, 70, 74
measure problem · 127
monkeys · 55, 57
multiverse · 141, 146

N

Newton, Isaac · 41, 72
non-overlapping
  magisteria · 102, 103

P

Plantinga, Alvin · 108, 109
Popper, Karl · 72
posterior probability · 21, 22, 23,
  24, 27, 36, 39, 50, 81
prior probability · 20, 23, 24, 25,
  27, 29, 36, 38, 40, 89, 97,
  111, 143, 144, 146, 147

problem of evil · 9, 10, 11

R

Roadrunner example · 115, 116,
  117

S

second law of
  thermodynamics · 105, 107
Strevens, Michael · 31, 97

T

Tiktaalik · 61
transmogrification · 121

U

unification of forces · 139

www.ingramcontent.com/pod-product-compliance
Lightning Source LLC
Chambersburg PA
CBHW060608080526
44585CB00013B/740